SHOTGUNS
AND
SHOOTING

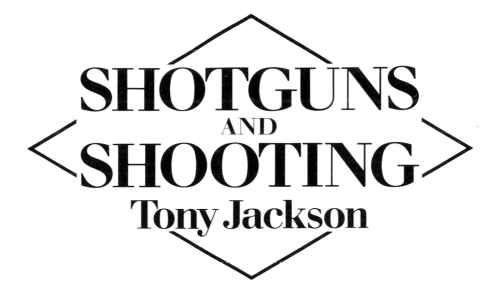

SHOTGUNS
AND
SHOOTING
Tony Jackson

Ward Lock Limited · London

Acknowledgments

The author and publishers would like to thank the following for kindly providing photographs for the book: Bath Press Photo Services page 19; G. Boothroyd pages 23, 24 top; G. L. Carlisle pages 52, 61 top and bottom, 70, 74; R. E. Chaplin page 63; N. J. L. Cotterell page 24 bottom; J. Good page 68; David Gowans page 57; Pamela Harrison page 53; Tony Jackson pages 40-42, 47 bottom, 48, 72; David de Lossy page 69; John Marchington pages 9, 12, 15, 17, 31, 47, 59, 79 top and bottom; Arthur Oglesby page 54; John A. Pearce page 20; S. C. Porter page 76; John Tarlton page 8.

Front jacket photograph by Dave Parfitt

Line drawings by Feref Associates Ltd

© Tony Jackson   1982

First published in Great Britain in 1982
by Ward Lock Limited, 82 Gower Street,
London WC1E 6EQ, a Pentos Company.

Designed by Charlotte Westbrook

Text filmset in 10 point Melior

Set, printed and bound in Great Britain by Netherwood Dalton and Co. Ltd.

British Library Cataloguing in Publication Data

Jackson, Tony
    Shotguns and shooting for beginners.
    1. Hunting—Great Britain—Amateurs' manuals
    I. Title
    799.2'13'0941   SK185

ISBN 0-7063-6173-3

Contents

Foreword 6

1 Shooting in the UK 7

2 Somewhere to shoot 14

3 Shotguns 22

4 Cartridges 28

5 Buying a gun 35

6 Safety 38

7 How to shoot 45

8 The law 50

9 Game 56

10 Wildfowl 67

11 Rabbits, pigeon and various 71

12 Gundogs 78

13 Clothing and equipment 83

Useful addresses 87

Index 91

Foreword

Despite claims to the contrary from the vociferous minority who would prefer to see them all banned, field sports today are thriving. The odds, theoretically, are against their advancement – a countryside which is being swiftly eroded, pollution and the unpleasing effects of man's indifference to his environment, all these plus the condemnation of the ignorant should, long since, have sounded the death knell for hunting, shooting and fishing. Curiously, the greater the clamour, the more interest taken in these traditional, legal and disciplined field sports.

Shooting has never been more popular, but inevitably the majority taking up the sport no longer have the benefit of a sporting family tradition. They must learn the hard way, a road which is, today, increasingly fraught with problems. This book, then, is for the complete beginner, the man or woman who has a hankering for the countryside and its sports. No attempt has been made to assume even basic knowledge on the part of the beginner.

A final thought – shooting is all about self-discipline and restraint. Perhaps when you've read this book you will begin to understand why.

1
Shooting in the UK

The acknowledged fact that Great Britain, despite its geographical restrictions and over-large population, still has some of the finest and most sought-after shooting in the world, is no mere chance of fate but a happy combination of history and politics. The development of the sporting gun, from flintlock to percussion and, finally, breechloader, closely followed changing patterns of agriculture and farming practice, whilst the private ownership of land and the geographical patterns of that land itself have ensured a generally flourishing and carefully managed variety of game.

Private land ownership has, of course, proved the crucial factor. One has only to consider countries where a communal, or free-for-all system has prevailed, to realize how fortunate we are in this respect. No one is going to take the trouble to preserve game if, at the end of the day, a stranger is likely to reap the rewards.

Our grouse moors, our pheasant coverts and our partridge manors have without exception been the envy of the world and it is little wonder that foreigners flock to Britain during the shooting season, only too delighted to pay a high price, realizing that in return they will enjoy the very best sport.

The game populations in Great Britain – with one exception – are probably as high, or higher, than they have ever been. Of course, there are fluctuations caused through disease or bad weather, nevertheless the grouse moors still flourish, whilst the pheasant population, enormously reinforced by rearing schemes, continues to provide the bread-and-butter of the game-shooting world. The one exception to this healthy picture is the grey partridge whose fortunes have tumbled and declined since World War II largely as the result of a drastically altered farming practice, resulting in the destruction of hedgerows and nesting cover, and the increased use of pesticides, coupled with a series of disastrous rearing seasons. The days when grey partridges provided the most superlative shooting on the manors of East Anglia through September and October will probably never be seen again. Its diminished numbers are now heavily supplemented by red-legged partridges which themselves have to be treated, rather like

Well-driven partridges can provide superlative sport.

pheasants, on a put-and-take basis. The red-leg, useful though it may be, lacks the verve and excitement of the grey bird.

Of duck, geese and waders the only fluctuations are likely to be brought about through bad weather, either during the breeding season or in the winter. Wildfowling is an exceptionally exciting sport and though the old days, when anyone could pick up a gun and wander onto the foreshore in search of a duck, are gone, the sport is still to be found, even if more regimented. The Wildfowlers' Association of Great Britain and Ireland (WAGBI), founded in 1908, deserves the thanks of all those who have the welfare of wildfowl at heart, whether they pursue them with gun or binoculars. Now WAGBI no longer exists, having been reborn as the British Association for Shooting and Conservation (BASC), but their splendid work continues, ensuring that the sport, whether on foreshore or inland, continues to flourish.

And what of our lesser sport? Well, now that the vile disease myxomatosis has declined, only flickering like a guttering candle in the autumn, rabbits are once again providing a wealth of opportunities, from ferreting, long-netting, wiring, stalking with a .22 rifle or just plain fun with a springer spaniel as they bolt from the scrub. Never despise the rabbit! Excellent food, in itself adaptable and versatile despite the worst that man can do to it, the rabbit can teach the beginner more about shooting and country craft than all the pheasants in Christendom. It may look simple, it may look soft, but believe me the coney knows exactly what it's up to. When man has wiped himself from the face of the earth, I have not the slightest doubt that from somewhere, once the smoke has cleared and the dust settled, a rabbit will emerge, cleaning its whiskers and looking for a mate!

Wildfowling is an exceptionally exciting sport.

Woodpigeon, too, still offer good sport and though their numbers declined in the seventies, respectable bags are once again being reported. In many areas, though, it appears that the flocks have become decoy wary, so the pigeon punisher really cannot leave anything to chance. Every aspect of the game must be studied if one is going to fill the car boot with 100-plus pigeon.

This book has been written for the complete novice, the raw beginner, and assumes that he or she lacks that most desirable of all commodities, a bottomless purse. If you can afford to purchase a gun in a syndicate, well and good, and if you can also afford a pair of guns, shooting lessons and the advice and company of a knowledgeable shooting man, your battle is virtually won. Such members of the shooting community are, perhaps, to be envied, yet they miss the best part of shooting, the involvement at a lower level which can be so rewarding. The man who runs his own tiny shoot, rearing perhaps 150 or 200 pheasants, learns more and, ultimately, has a far greater reward than he who simply buys a gun in a shoot and takes no interest in its organization throughout the year.

Pheasant shooting, as I remarked before, is the backbone of game shooting in this country. The private shoots that flourished until World War II can still be found, though their numbers are diminishing. They are overshadowed by the syndicate shoots which, in a variety of guises, are to be found throughout the length and breadth of the land. Birds reared may range from a modest fifty or so to several thousand, supplemented, quite frequently, by partridges and duck. The variations on the theme are numerous, the type of land usually dictating the shooting. I would always prefer a small day with a variety of game to the pheasant-only battue where perhaps 300 to 1,000 or more birds are killed in a day. They may be, and we hope are, high, fast and sporting, but I would still prefer to shoot a handful of pheasants, some partridges, a few duck, rabbits and pigeon, with perhaps a woodcock thrown in for good measure. That sort of day will have provided a wealth of colour and excitement. I have nothing against big bags provided the birds have been sporting, but my inclination is towards the more informal approach – particularly if I can use my own dogs.

Possibly the most exciting bird of all to shoot is the grouse. A driving moor in August, the burning sun lighting the purple-clad hillsides, the scent of heather and hum of bees as the birds skim the contours, flashing over the line of butts, is an experience never to be forgotten. Grouse are mostly associated with the moors of Scotland and Yorkshire yet they are to be found in Wales, as far south as Shropshire, and there are even a handful still eking out a precarious existence in the West Country.

What of the other species of grouse in the country? Blackgame are widely spread in the north of England and Scotland and anyone who has had the fortune to shoot a blackcock (the female is called a greyhen) will agree that it is a truly magnificent bird with its black plumage, red wattles and lyre-shaped tail. Surprisingly fast, blackgame will usually be found in birch and rowan-dotted dells and ghylls on the edge of the moors.

Their big brother, the capercaillie, the largest grouse, is to be found only in Scotland where, thanks to the spread of forestry and the sensible protection now afforded them by the Forestry Commission, their future seems well assured. They were, in fact, reduced to extinction in the latter part of the eighteenth century, only being re-established by an introduction of stock from Sweden in the early part of the following century.

A driven capercaillie is an awe-inspiring sight. Weighing perhaps 10 or 12 lb (4.5 – 5.4 kg), it races downhill at incredible speed, the wings set, merely giving a flicker now and then.

The final grouse is the ptarmigan, a bird of the high tops. Rarely found under the 2,000 ft (600 m) mark, and only in Scotland, ptarmigan demand a special expedition for their capture and are seldom, if ever, found in the bag as part of a day's general sport. Delightful birds, they have four plumage phases through the year, the most handsome being in the winter when, with their snow-white feathers, relieved only by red wattles and black outer tail feathers, they are trophies worthy of a glass case.

Owing to the mountainous regions they inhabit, ptarmigan can never be deliberately driven over waiting guns. Erupting suddenly from grey, lichen-covered rocks to glide on stiff-pinioned wings, they are a truly wild bird, only to be sought by those who are prepared to climb and walk long distances. Their camouflage is incredibly efficient. It is quite possible to walk within a few yards of the birds, totally unaware of their presence until, suddenly, the ground apparently explodes as the beautifully-marked birds flicker up and away.

The duck and geese of this country demand, if one is to come to grips with them, a solitary approach and the exercise of considerable field craft. I am talking here of truly wild fowl, the majority of which are winter migrants to Britain from the more northerly parts of Europe, Russia and Iceland. Reared mallard, now a regular asset on many shoots, can provide excellent shooting, but are to be treated largely as one treats driven pheasants.

It is now virtually impossible for the individual who decides to pursue the ancient craft of wildfowling, just to pick up his gun and descend on to the foreshore. This was once the case in England and Wales, for the Crown owns the greater part of the foreshore and although one was technically trespassing, a blind eye was turned. Unfortunately, the situation got out of hand in the 1950s and 1960s as wildfowling increased in popularity. An irresponsible element – marsh cowboys – started to give wildfowling a very bad name; protected birds were shot and out-of-range shooting became commonplace. Fortunately, WAGBI (as it then was) stepped in to negotiate an agreement whereby only members of WAGBI-affiliated clubs could enjoy the privileges of the foreshore. Largely speaking, clubs now control virtually the entire foreshore, though by no means is the entire area available for shooting as most clubs set aside reserves, or work in conjunction with local nature conservation or bird societies to provide areas for breeding where birds will not be disturbed.

In Scotland the situation is somewhat different as here there exists an historical right of access to the foreshore. However, once again clubs have been formed to cover the principle areas of importance, so that access to shoot is only by membership.

Despite the responsible attitude adopted by the BASC and its associate clubs and members, there are still today far too many so-called wildfowlers who, once on the foreshore, seem to assume that anything goes. The Solway and the Wash, both still meccas for the fowler, are plagued by 'cowboys' who, it seems, are quite incapable of judging the height of a goose or duck or who have no idea of the killing pattern and range of their

Rough shooting — a spaniel hunting for rabbits in bracken.

guns. Stories of geese shot at 80 to 100 yd (70 – 90 m) are common, but these are only stories. Unfortunately, just occasionally an unlucky goose is dropped by a stray pellet, even though the bird was way out of normal range. Its demise is seen by those who know no better and so the wretched practice is perpetuated.

Driven shooting, wildfowling . . . but what of rough shooting? This is probably the branch of shooting practised by the majority of sportsmen. And what is rough shooting? Well, if you pick up your gun and wander out in the evening with the old spaniel for a rabbit, if two or three of you walk up your shoot for the odd pheasant, duck or partridge, if you wait by a pool or stream in the evening for a duck, then you are a rough shooter. Any aspect of shooting that is not driven, wildfowling proper or pigeon shooting with a purpose, falls into this category.

Shooting is, today, despite the doom and gloom, in a remarkably healthy frame of mind. Perhaps our greatest asset is a natural inclination towards responsible management and a realization that the resource must be husbanded. One has only to look to certain areas of the Continent – one thinks in particular of Italy – to realize how swiftly an unthinking and greedy approach to shooting can lead to a denuded wasteland.

Our chief problem is to accommodate the increasing numbers who have a desire to establish a stake in the countryside and engage in its field sports. It can be done, however, and the next chapter will tell you how.

2
Somewhere to shoot

The difficulties associated with finding somewhere to shoot, or simply taking one's first tentative steps into the shooting field, are related to one's degree of access to the countryside. In broad terms, and assuming you are not in a position to buy your way in, then the more slender your connections with the rural landscape, the more difficult the whole business becomes – if you live in the middle of London you're going to have to work a darn sight harder than the lucky fellow who commutes from a Sussex village. But, as with most things, rewards are commensurate with the effort involved.

At the top end of the shooting scale, and assuming you are sufficiently well breeched, one can simply purchase a gun in a syndicate, take some shooting lessons and, hey presto! you're an instant shooting man . . . or you may like to think you are! If that's your lucky situation you probably won't be reading this book, so we'll drop down a peg or two.

Guns can, of course, still be bought in modest little shoots for an outlay of about £200 – £400 for the season. These are frequently excellent value. The sport may be a combination of driven and rough shooting but if you have chosen well and your associate guns are congenial you may well enjoy some first-class days. Most shoots of this nature, perhaps rearing 200 or 300 pheasants, a few duck and, possibly, some partridges, will shoot eight to ten days during the season and may well have arrangements for pigeon flighting and rabbiting in the close season. A responsible, well-trained dog is always an asset and invariably welcomed . . . an unruly, ill-mannered brute is not and is quite likely to lead to a swift termination of your association with the shoot. Guns available in shoots of this nature are regularly advertised in the shooting and country magazines. But, beware! It's very much a case of *caveat emptor* . . . let the buyer take heed. Before signing your cheque certain precautions must be taken.

The first thing is, obviously, to acquire a full verbal description of the shoot from the organizer. If the acreage is small be very cautious. Anything under 300 acres calls for deep probing. It may well be that a very small

Note the farming policy . . . a purpose-planted pheasant covert with a windbreak.

acreage has some noteworthy asset, such as one or more ponds or lakes which offer fine duck shooting, or the geography is such that a great many birds can be held on a relatively modest amount of land. But it could also be a nasty fifty or 100 acres of forestry which, whilst it may have held birds in its youth, has now become a gloomy shelter for roosting pigeon and little else.

Obviously you must insist on visiting the shoot. Take note of the farming policy. If you can confirm small fields, large overgrown hedges, six- or seven-acre spinneys with plenty of light, good bottoms and warm shelter belts, plus the occasional ducky pool and a farmer who is only too pleased to co-operate by way of providing game belts, labour and enthusiasm, then you are certainly on a likely winner . . . and unbelievably fortunate!

If, on the other hand, you find yourself tramping across a windy, cold expanse of vast, empty fields with not a hedgerow or wood in sight, take a hard, second look. You may still be in luck. There are numerous shoots, many highly successful, in Cambridgeshire and Lincolnshire that may, at first sight, appear singularly unpropitious. But, sown with roots and kale,

15

such fields can produce some reasonable shooting, though the birds have to be driven some distance in order to gain height. There is little sport or satisfaction in shooting low pheasants out of kale, quite apart from the fact that it can be very dangerous.

Take careful note of the cropping rotation. Is the entire farm down to grain or is there a mixture of grain, roots and grass? Does the farmer run a beef or dairy herd and if so what acreage of kale does he grow?

Look carefully at the woods. Are the rides clean and tidy? Can you see feed hoppers dotted strategically and is there a trace of straw in the rides where winter feed has been scattered? Ask to see the release pen or pens. Make sure they look firm and sound, with stout posts, and the wire well dug in and floppy round the top to prevent foxes helping themselves. Is there an electric wire round the perimeter of the pen as a fox deterrent?

A well-run release wood should look clean, smart and efficient. One does not want to see remnants of old pens rotting in the wood or scattered sheets of galvanized iron. Watch out for signs of rats and ask to see a few of the tunnel traps which should be set for vermin. And whilst on this subject ascertain the shoot owner's policy towards vermin and predators. Rats, stoats, weasels, crows and magpies must be controlled, but there is no excuse for the man who deliberately makes war against protected species such as owls and hawks. It may be considered knowing or smart by the unthinking to poison, shoot or trap these creatures on the spurious pretext that they are likely to harm our interests, but today there is room for predatory birds that were once anathema to the keeper. Remember that it is *we* who have created an imbalance in nature by artificially rearing birds and introducing them into the countryside on a massive scale. I am perfectly well aware that a sparrowhawk may take a few pheasants or partridge chicks but I would still rather see that dashing buccaneer on my shoot and shoot perhaps a handful less birds.

What of foxes? I hope that you will agree that all field sports share a common heritage and use of the countryside. No keeper requires a fox in his rearing pen, but close collaboration with the local hunt will ensure that the problem is kept to a minimum. Be wary of the owner or manager, then, who tells you with a nudge and a wink that not a fox lives on the farm. If this is the case, you may be sure that his reputation in the district is none too high and by associating with him you may do yourself little good.

Boundaries are extremely important. Ascertain, firstly, the shooting policies, if any, of the neighbouring estates. You may find that one farm bordering perhaps three-quarters of the shoot has a massive rearing policy. If this is the case, discreet enquiry will disclose whether your potential shoot owner adopts the policy of helping himself. In other words, does he site game crops along the boundary and try to feed in birds from his

Check the release pen. Note the electric 'anti-fox' fence.

neighbour? If so you may be sure that considerable friction will exist, not unnaturally, between the two estates and you may find yourself in the middle of a 'range war'. On the other hand, you can easily find yourself on the receiving end with a greedy, inconsiderate neighbour who is drawing off the birds from your shoot.

If you feel that the shoot is to your liking, and assuming that you in turn are accepted, you can then enquire rather more closely into the small print. Find out, for instance, on what terms the lease is arranged. If it is on an annual basis you should be cautious. Such a lease may indicate that the farmer or landowner is not prepared to accept continuity and there is little likelihood that the shoot itself will be run on established, long-term lines. One would prefer to know that the lease is at least three years, but preferably seven. Make sure that your subscription covers the cost of beaters and that you are not expected to pay for them on each day's shooting.

A small shoot up to 1,000 acres and rearing up to the same number of birds is unlikely today to employ a full-time keeper. Most shoots accept the services of a part-timer, who may be employed on the farm, or has a free gun in the shoot for his services. There are numerous variations on the small shoot theme; for instance, to keep down costs you may be asked to assist with rearing if you have the facilities, or to do work on the shoot in the summer. It's very much a case of making your choice and paying your money.

All the above, and it applies equally if you are renting a shoot, assumes that you are willing to pay several hundred pounds each season.

You may, however, for various reasons prefer to keep your costs to an absolute minimum. Shooting can still be obtained for virtually now't but it's becoming increasingly more difficult. Like all things in life, approach and first appearances count for a great deal. So let's examine ways of obtaining an entry into the shooting field for the cost, perhaps, only of your petrol.

If you live in a town or city or have recently moved into the country, the first thing is to define your objectives. Perhaps you imagine that you are going to acquire permission to shoot over several hundred acres, for game and what-have-you, merely by asking politely . . . forget it! Those days are long vanished. Twenty or thirty years ago shooting could be had for the asking and a bottle of whisky or brace of pheasants at Christmas. Now every farmer is well aware of its value. Only in the most remote regions, in farthest Scotland or Wales, can one still obtain rough shooting for little cost.

On the other hand your ambitions at this stage may rise no higher than pigeon or rabbits. Again, do not imagine that you are doing the farmer a favour by offering to control them. Although some farmers may appear singularly dog-in-the-mangerish, complaining bitterly that they are over-run with rabbits yet refusing you permission, on the whole they know exactly to whom to turn . . . and it's very unlikely to be the first person who comes knocking at the door.

Having said that, it is still perfectly feasible to obtain pigeon and rabbit shooting for little, or no cost, provided the right approach is taken and the preliminary groundwork carefully planned. It is a total waste of time and petrol to drive from farm to farm, the car laden with decoys, nets and guns and a couple of spaniels in the back, and to expect a farmer, land-owner or keeper to give you permission to shoot. Pigeon may be beating hell out of the barley, rabbits may be queueing up for the greenstuff, but nobody in his right mind is today going to allow an armed stranger on his land without knowing a great deal about his background and credentials. Permission, given on the spur of the moment, may later be regretted as the game population suddenly dwindles!

All right, we know that you would never make a false move, that you would conscientiously shut gates and ensure that stock is enclosed, that you would pick up all your empty cartridge cases and tidy up your hide – but does the farmer know? Besides, in the majority of cases the farmer is unlikely to be in a position to give permission. When the sporting rights have already been let, he can only allow certain members of his staff and family to shoot the ground game, i.e., hares and rabbits (see Chapter 8), and that permission must be in writing. The odds are that in the majority of cases the pigeon and rabbit shooting has already been acquired, quite often by a local club on whose services the farmer knows he can rely in an emergency.

So, what can be done? Whether you have to travel to the country, or live in a rural community, the one centre of information, the citizens' advice bureau of the sporting world, is the local inn. Here you will find, in the

Pigeon shooting can be obtained for little cost.

Volunteer your services as a beater.

public bar, all the local worthies. The big problem, once you have wangled your way into their confidences via a few pints, is sorting the wheat from the chaff! Try to meet the local keeper; sporting news and life, if he is the right sort – and not a teetotaller – will tend to centre on his activities. If you are accepted, you will soon learn the geography of the area, who owns what, where pigeon are moving, how game is faring, and so on. You may strike lucky, provided you play your cards right and don't try to be too pushy, and get the odd invitation to flight pigeon or assist with a Sunday morning's ferreting. If this fails, volunteer your services in the shooting season as a beater on a local estate. The advantages are many. Not only will you be paid and receive some vigorous exercise, but you will learn a great deal about shooting from the blunt end and, vital from your point of view, once it is established that you're keen and willing to learn, you will almost certainly receive invitations to vermin and pigeon shoots when the season is over. Thereafter, it's up to you.

An alternative approach, or one to be used in conjunction with the foregoing method, is to join your nearest BASC club. Such clubs vary in their scope. They range from major wildfowling clubs, sited on important, coastal areas, to inland rough shooting clubs or pigeon and rabbit clearance societies. However, if they have good sport and their own club shoot, there will certainly be a waiting list, with preferential treatment given to locals, which is only reasonable.

Failing this, and despite the fact that you may have no particular interest in shooting targets, your nearest clay club has several advantages. Firstly, you are going to be taught how to shoot moving targets . . . and shoot them safely. A year's regular weekly attendance at such a club, preferably one with a sporting layout, will give you confidence and ensure your acceptance in any company. Furthermore, you will be meeting shooting men who may prove valuable contacts in the world of live shooting. The BASC run a series of extremely useful courses for beginners in every aspect of shooting — safety, identification, and so on, and these are thoroughly recommended. Taken in conjunction with the services of a clay club you will have acquired an established and proven background. And there is another spin off. You may quite likely become a clay afficionado!

I repeat, if you are quite determined to obtain your own pigeon or rabbit shooting, or even better your own small shoot, which you can build up, perhaps with the aid of a few selected friends, you must first gain at least a rudimentary working knowledge of the countryside and how shooting works. Put aside a year in which to learn how to shoot and all the safety rules, and in which to make your contacts. Then go all out for your own shoot.

Be prepared to travel, follow up the most unlikely leads and never be disheartened. I receive a considerable volume of correspondence from readers who complain that their utmost efforts bring them no joy. I just don't believe it. If you approach people correctly, take time to study a situation and don't rush in baldheaded expecting to be offered shooting on a plate, then eventually you must succeed. There is still shooting to be found, even close to London, but you have to use your eyes to find it.

3
Shotguns

You will be pleased to know that I am not, definitely not, a ballistician nor am I what is termed, Stateside, a gun bug. I enjoy handling a well-made, finely balanced shotgun and I know and understand its inherent qualities. However, a gun is still a tool to perform a service, efficiently and at my behest. Don't let yourself be baffled by 'gunnitis', by the more mysterious applications of raised ventilated ribs, poly-chokes and Monte Carlo stocks. These are alleged refinements which will do little to assist the beginner.

The basic types of shotgun may be divided into the conventional drop-down guns, either side-by-side or over-and-under, the repeaters, which includes the manually-operated repeaters such as the slide-action or pump-gun; the recoil-operated automatics and the gas-operated automatics. Lastly can be included the bolt-action which, though it has a poor rate of fire, usually encompasses within its slim lines, good balance and handling qualities.

The repeaters, five or three shot, are of American origin and none the worse for that. Rugged, hard-wearing, they will provide years of service but are quite unsuitable for the complete beginner as their handling qualities leave much to be desired. Because of the forward disposition of their weight, the balance is poor and they are likely to incline a novice shot towards that most fatal of shooting malignancies, a tendency to poke. Remington, Winchester and Browning have each produced excellent guns in a variety of grades but compared with the utility, ease of loading, balance and looks of a conventional side-by-side, the latter wins hands down.

However, one must always remember the ancient precept – that the best gun for a man is the one with which he shoots best. If you find that you can cope with a repeater and that its qualities meet your demands then don't be deterred. Recall, though, that a repeater is not welcome in game circles, if you intend to shoot in company. This is not just tradition but is based on practical considerations. It is, for example, impossible to tell whether an automatic is loaded or empty, its capacity for five cartridges may indicate a certain greed, whilst its basically unpleasing lines clash with the conventional shooting field. You may not agree with these precepts, but that's the way it's been done for decades and that's the way it will continue.

By now, you may have caught on to the notion that I prefer a drop-down game gun, and of the alternatives available I prefer, every time, the side-by-side to the over-and-under. Let me quickly tell you why. The side-by-side has stood the test of time and emerged unscathed. The sidelock or boxlock which we shoot today is fundamentally exactly the same gun as our forebears used with eminent success in the 1880s and 1890s. Delightfully balanced, easy to manipulate, i.e., to load and unload, the side-by-side game gun has all the graces and points of the thoroughbred. It will do the job required of it to perfection and no one can ask more than that. The over-and-under seems to be an unnecessary variation on a tried and proven theme. Its very construction, the barrels placed one on top of the other, demands a depth in the action which can cause difficulty when loading and unloading, whilst trouble with ejectors is not unknown. Early over-and-unders were extremely ungainly, lacking in grace and style, but experiments by Boss and Woodward went a long way to obviate this fault, whilst in 1926 Browning introduced their 'superpose' which was the first of the really modern over-and-unders. Extremely popular with clay busters and

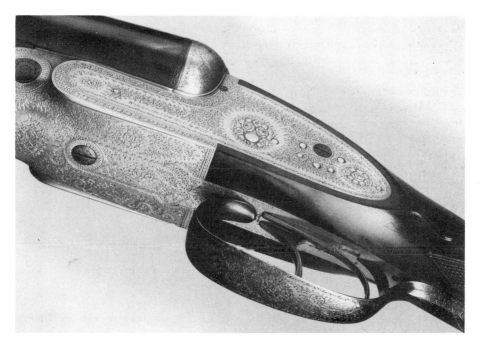

A superb side-by-side 12 bore by William Powell & Sons.

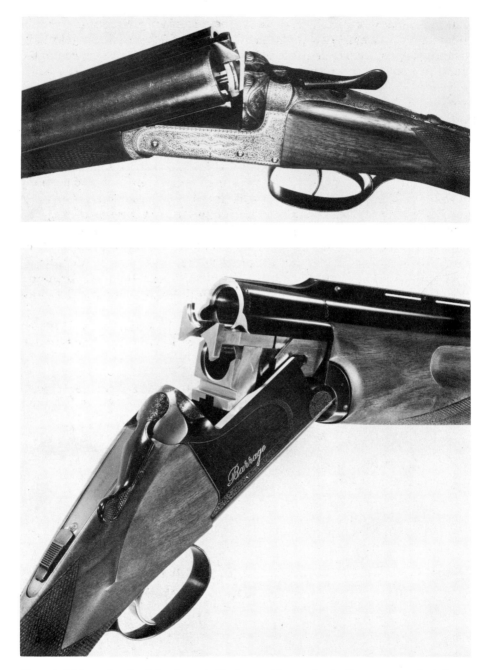

Top: *A 20 bore boxlock by Joseph Harkom. Above: An Italian over-and-under.*

seen increasingly in the field, there can be no denying that the over-and-under now has an established place in the market. Yet I still do not take to it because of the aforementioned loading problem, though this should not be over-emphasized, and in particular because of the single-sighting plane. However, this is a grievance which may be common to those who have been reared on a side-by-side and the beginner coming straight to the over-and-under may well adapt to its style.

Before we choose a gun, however, let's just work our way round a conventional side-by-side and examine its basic components. The barrels are, simply, cylindrical steel tubes into which the cartridges are inserted and through which the shot charge is conveyed. The length of the barrels, for game and rough shooting, is today likely to be 28 in (710 mm); 30 in (760 mm) barrels are now considered old-fashioned, whilst there was a rage in the 1920s – and one recently revived – for ultra-short barrels of 25 in (635 mm). The size of a shotgun's bore is denoted by the figure 12, 16, 20, 28 or .410. This indicates that, in the case of a 12-bore, twelve spherical balls of pure lead weighing 1 lb (.450 g) in total would each exactly fit the diameter of that bore. The .410 is the odd man out, as any bore smaller than a 32-bore is measured in decimels.

The chamber of the gun is the slightly enlarged section into which the cartridges are inserted. The chamber is connected to the bore by a tapered cone.

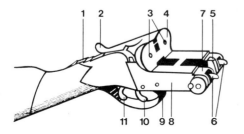

Action 1. safety catch; 2. lever; 3. strikers; 4. action face; 5. extractor cam; 6. cocking levers; 7. knuckle; 8. side plate; 9. trigger guard; 10. right trigger; 11. left trigger.

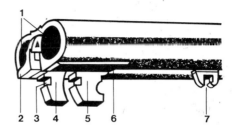

Barrels 1. breech; 2. extractor; 3. bite; 4. rear lump; 5. hook; 6. flat; 7. bolt loop.

The parts of a side-by-side shotgun.

The fore-end is the length of wood which clips underneath the barrels, usually being held in place by a snap spring bolt, known as a push-rod bolt, or, in older guns, a lever which is pushed to one side. The fore-end will also enclose the ejector tumblers and the recesses for the cocking levers.

The action consists of the mechanism for firing the cartridges. Basically there are two types of action – the sidelock and the boxlock, though there is a third, the Dickson's round action, which is less likely to be encountered.

The boxlock is the commonest type of action; easily adjusted, it fits into a solid action body, the springs running underneath the action. One can readily recognize a boxlock by the fact that it lacks the oval plates on either side of the action which is the mark of the sidelock. Lines, too, will indicate a slightly bulkier gun.

In the sidelock, the lock work is mounted on removable plates in the side of the action. A more intricate and expensive system, it is seen in the very best quality game guns. I would, however, prefer a cheap boxlock to a cheap sidelock for obvious reasons.

The gun will normally be opened by a lever placed on top of the action; by pushing this to one side the barrels can be lowered and in some expensive guns an easy opening action is a self-explanatory refinement. The lever may also, on older guns, be found on the side of the action or under it.

The usual game gun has two triggers. The front one activates the right-hand barrel and the back the left barrel. The reason for this order of fire is an assumption that the first barrel will be fired at a close target and the second at the same target, in the case of a miss, it by now being further away. In the case of a kill with the first barrel the second will be available for a more distant target. But why the difference? Why should both barrels not have the same killing range? The answer lies in one word – choke.

Choke consists of a constriction in the end of the barrel, so that the charge of shot, ejected from the cartridge into a cylinder, is suddenly squeezed as it is forced by impelling gases through the abruptly narrowed barrel. Imagine, if you will, the effect of constricting the end of a hosepipe; from a lavish spread of water one can suddenly obtain a thin, powerful jet. It is much the same with shot. We'll take a look at cartridge and shot patterns in the next chapter.

The stock is the wooden section attached to the action and can be made in a variety of shapes, though the most common is the straight hand, the type of stock normally used for game and rough shooting. The half or full pistol-gripped stocks are encountered on heavy wildfowling guns or clay trap guns, whilst another variation, the Monte Carlo stock, is also used for trap shooting.

The safety catch is situated behind the top lever on the grip or hand of the stock and it is important to note that the safety catch will prevent the triggers from being pulled but it does not control the action of the gun. Thus it is possible, where the sears are worn, for a gun to be fired, perhaps through inadvertently dropping it, even though the safety catch is on. Remember that gun safety comes before reliance on the safety catch.

A type of safety catch which I dislike intensely, and which is usually found on over-and-unders, is the non-automatic or manual safety. In other words, every time the gun is fired the safety has to be operated by the shooter; it is all too easy to forget this simple action in the heat of the moment.

As a beginner, do not concern or worry yourself with the esoteric aspects of shotguns. Raised, ventilated ribs, polychokes, chrome-plated barrels, these are not for you to worry about or concern yourself with. I am a firm believer in starting on the right foot, which, for a beginner who has not yet decided which branch of the shooting sport he is likely to follow, is a side-by-side 12-bore, either a boxlock or sidelock, ejector or non-ejector. A sidelock ejector is to be preferred if the piggy bank will stand it, but there is absolutely nothing wrong with a well-made boxlock and if it is a non-ejector, well, you'll just have to remove the spent cartridges by hand.

Once you have obtained experience, some skill and have seen a variety of guns being used for a variety of purposes, you may decide that you want to change. It's surprising, though, the number of people who, having sampled over-and-unders, repeaters and lord knows what, ultimately return to the classic side-by-side.

The side-by-side can do anything that the others can do and with rather more style. You will, of course, today never see a clay shot with anything other than an over-and-under, but Percy Stanbury, one of the greatest shots of all time and a professional coach, won virtually every championship going with a Webley side-by-side. However, he used a five-shot auto when he performed his incredible feat of killing five woodpigeon and having all five dead in the air at the same time!

4
Cartridges

The modern cartridge consists of a plastic tube which acts as a container for the charge of lead pellets which comprise the shot, for the powder and for the wad which separates the two; also included in the case is the brass head which contains a non-corrosive cap, or primer. Today's cartridge must be waterproof, an attribute sadly lacking in the old paper cases which would swell at the slightest hint of moisture, rendering them impossible to force into the chambers of the gun.

The cartridge case has two other functions: it must hold the shot until the powder is fully ignited, so that the charge receives maximum pressures from the gases and, most important of all, it must seal the breech against the pressure of those gases.

Let's look at the operation of a cartridge. The cap, inserted into the brass head of the cartridge, is struck by the firing-pin. The blow detonates the compound in the cap and the searing flame released in turn ignites the powder. Today this will be a nitro-cellulose compound which will be graded according to its speed of burning. Thus it is usual for slow-burning powders to be used in conjunction with magnum loads and fast-burning powders with high-velocity light charges.

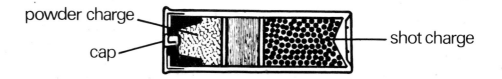

powder charge — cap — shot charge

The basic components of a cartridge.

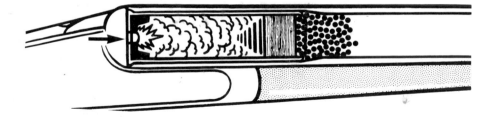

A cartridge detonated in the chamber of a shotgun.

The gases from the burning powder now drive the wad and charge of lead pellets, impelling the crimp closure at the front of the cartridge to open and thus release them into the barrel. It is the wad's job to seal the bore, ensuring that no gases leak past and disrupt the charge of shot. If this doe occ r the pattern of shot will be badly disfigured or blown.

The shot itself consists of so-called 'chilled' lead, which is harder than pure lead and comprises an alloy of lead-arsenic-antimony. Such shot is made by dropping molten lead from a sieve at the top of a high tower into water.

Our charge of shot, consisting perhaps of 1 oz (28 g) of No 6 shot, a total of 287 pellets, is now hurtling down the barrel, to meet a degree of choke which, as explained previously, will have the effect of constricting the mass of pellets. The degree of constriction will depend on the amount of choke. A fully choked barrel will produce a much tighter pattern than one with a quarter choke or virtually no choke at all. The latter is called a true cylinder.

We will come back to this in a moment. The pattern produced by the charge of shot is normally measured as a 30 in (760 mm) circle at a distance of 40 yd (35 m). What we are looking for is a balanced, even pattern, lacking the blank spaces through which a bird might fly unscathed, nor do we want tight clusters of pellets, balling or sticking together.

The beginner is frequently attracted to the notion of full choke. The tighter the choke, he reasons, the greater will be the number of pellets he can cram into the 30 in (760 mm) circle and thus the more likely is it that a bird will be mortally hit. But he forgets that by far the majority of shots, taken at a variety of game, are within the 20 to 25 yd (18 – 23 m) bracket and at that range the degree of aiming error is increased as the pattern is tightened. The larger and more even the pattern, the greater the chance of striking a quarry with the minimum three or four pellets. Choke is a snare and a delusion. The average game gun will be bored right barrel improved cylinder, and left barrel half or three-quarter choke, half choke being preferable. The other great drawback of full choke is that at normal ranges game will be badly smashed through a surfeit of unnecessary pellets. Full choke will make you extremely unpopular with the cook.

This does not mean that choke can be entirely dispensed with. The wildfowler on the foreshore, dealing with geese or duck at maximum range, will make good use of choke; his shots may be taken at 40 to 45 yd (35 − 40 m) and at this range full choke with a heavy charge, say $1\frac{1}{2}$ oz (42 g) of No 4 or No 1 shot, will do the trick.

The normal game load in a 12-bore is $1\frac{1}{6}$ oz (30 g) or $1\frac{1}{8}$ oz (32 g) in a $2\frac{1}{2}$ in (63 mm) case. This can, however, be misleading as due to modern crimp closures the $2\frac{1}{2}$ in (63 mm) case is just over 2 in (50 mm) long, whilst the $2\frac{3}{4}$ in (70 mm) case may well fit inside a gun proved only for a $2\frac{1}{2}$ in (63 mm) case. It is vital, therefore, that you know to what load your gun has been proved and that you check that the cartridges you are using are suitable for that gun.

Shot is graded according to its size. The higher the number the smaller the shot, thus we have dust shot which is minute, progressing down to No 6 shot which is a very popular size for most game shooting, No 4 or No 3, used for duck and geese and the really heavy loads such as No 1, BB, SSG, or LG. Obviously the smaller the shot, the greater the number that can be crammed into a load. It might be thought that the more, the merrier. Not so, because the lighter shot will have reduced velocity and killing power.

To simplify life the beginner should stick to 1 oz (28 g) or $1\frac{1}{16}$ oz (30 g) of No 6 or 7 shot for all-round shooting. He will not go far wrong and will be capable of coping, with one or two exceptions, with anything from snipe to a pheasant or inland duck. For geese or fowl shot under extreme conditions he must use larger shot and a heavier load. One exception to the No 6 shot rule, mentioned above, is the hare. It is a big, strong animal, and I would much prefer to use No 4 shot if I know that hares are likely to figure in the bag. Nothing is more unpleasant than having to deal with a wounded hare; wounded because it has been shot with unsuitable shot. Those who have heard an injured hare screaming pitifully will know precisely what I mean. I avoid shooting hares unless I particularly want one for the table. In the last few years the brown hare population has declined in some areas and, praise be, the late-winter hare shoots are seldom necessary. It was not so long ago that bags of several hundred hares in a day were commonplace; unfortunately, such shoots acted as a magnet for every local who owned a gun and the resultant standards of safety and acts of cruel and thoughtless shooting made the hare shoot an occasion to be avoided at all costs.

It is best to use No 4 shot for hare. Do not risk wounding them.

It is vital that the beginner should grasp an essential truth—it is not guns which kill, it is patterns. Every gun will have a favourite and effective diet, and to know what to feed it you must formulate a working knowledge of the patterns it throws with various makes and sizes of cartridge. As previously mentioned, the pattern is normally checked at a distance of 40 yd (35 m) when the spread of shot in a 30 in (760 mm) circle is assessed. In order to test the patterns thrown by your gun, use a 6 ft (1.8 m) square of whitewashed steel. Measure 40 yd (35 m) and, after firing one shot in the air to clear the barrel of oil, fire at the centre of the plate. By eye, estimate the centre of the pattern and then draw a 30 in (760 mm) circle round it. Count off the number of pellets in the circle and judge whether the pattern is evenly distributed. Are there any blank spaces through which a pigeon, snipe or duck could fly? Are there any clusters of shot leaving wide spaces? If so, this may be due to a badly loaded cartridge or to one which is too powerful for the gun.

By firing five cartridges and taking an average of the number of pellets, you will be able to work out the average percentage of pellets for the load in relation to the degree of choke.

The following table gives the percentage patterns of varying degrees of choke at four ranges.

Boring	Range			
	30 yd (27.5 m)	35 yd (32 m)	40 yd (36 m)	45 yd (41 m)
True cylinder	60	49	40	33
Improved cylinder	72	60	50	41
$\frac{1}{4}$ choke	77	65	55	46
$\frac{1}{2}$ choke	83	71	60	50
$\frac{3}{4}$ choke	91	77	65	55
Full choke	100	84	70	59

Now, before we become bogged down in a welter of tables and statistics, let's recap on the essentials. Try to bear in mind that you are aiming for an evenly distributed pattern and that this will be achieved within the 30 in (760 mm) circle by the least possible choke combined with a light load of No 6 or 7 shot. Treat with unqualified suspicion claims for the merits of heavy shot and full choke. For certain specified tasks it is an admirable combination but for all-round game and rough shooting it is a certain recipe for disaster.

Shotting patterns.

Game load
All 12 bore loads

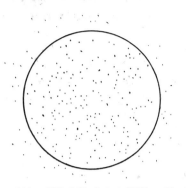

1⅛ oz (32 g). No 6 shot. 57% at 40 yd
(35 m). Half choke barrel.

Wildfowl load

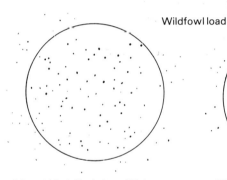

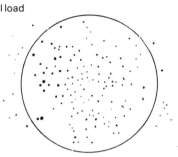

1½ oz (42 g). No 1 shot. 2¾ in
(70 mm) case. 58% at 40 yd (35 m).
Full choke barrel.

1½ oz (42 g). No 1 shot. 87% at 40 yd
(35 m). Full choke barrel.

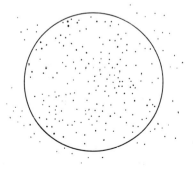

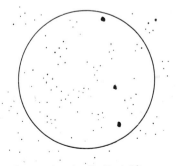

1⅛ oz (32 g). No 6 shot. 61% at 50 yd
(45 m). Full choke barrel.

Pattern showing 'balling'. 1¹/₁₆ oz
(30 g). No 6 shot. Improved cylinder
barrel.

Finally, under this section, the beginner should know something of proof. All shotguns have to be tested by the London or Birmingham Proof Houses in order to ensure that their barrels are capable of withstanding the pressures exerted by modern nitro powders.

It is of the utmost importance to understand that modern nitro powders must never be fired through the barrels of a gun which lacks nitro proof marks. There are, even today, elderly shotguns in circulation, perhaps 100 or more years old, which were built originally to fire black powder, a propellant which is far more forgiving than nitro powder, and to fire a modern cartridge through their ancient, perhaps damascus-steel barrels, is to court disaster. You may escape with a bulged barrel at best, at worst you could be seriously maimed by a bursting tube.

The proof marks of many foreign countries are accepted by the proof houses in this country and their guns do not require re-proof; there are others though, such as America, where there is no form of barrel proofing, whose guns must be proved in this country before they can be sold.

Proof marks are complex and demand, for their interpretation, the skills of a qualified gunsmith.

5
Buying a gun

The choice of a gun is all too frequently taken without a careful consideration of the long-term results. The two immediate problems facing the tyro seeking his first gun is choice and cost. If he has an open-ended cheque book the difficulties are at once reduced. He has merely to hie himself to a reputable gunmaker, explain his needs, the type of shooting he is most likely to be pursuing and how much he is prepared to pay. The rest is simple. He will soon be the proud owner of a quality game gun, almost certainly a sidelock ejector, which will have been adjusted to his physical requirements on the fitting range.

Such a gun may cost between £1,500 and £10,000, depending on its provenance and whether it is new or secondhand.

Let's suppose, however, that funds are restricted and you have a top figure of £700 or £800. You are looking for a well-balanced game gun, one that will pass in any company, a jack-of-all-work which you can use on the foreshore, for pigeon or a driven day at pheasants. For this sort of money one can still obtain an English boxlock but it will be secondhand and the pitfalls in buying secondhand guns are perfectly calculated to trap the unwary, though the element of risk can be reduced, as we shall see shortly. Good, sound English boxlocks, however, are becoming increasingly scarce, their place being taken by importations from Japan, Italy, France, a few of the Eastern bloc countries, and, of course, America.

Do not be put off by stories you may have heard concerning the iniquities of foreign guns. Certainly, a good many years ago, when the trickle suddenly became a deluge, the market was flooded with some very low-quality guns. However, that is now almost a thing of the past and the quality of guns, in particular from Italy and Spain, is extremely high. I have used a Spanish side-by-side ejector for twenty years and only once has it had to receive attention from the gunsmith, apart from its regular servicing. The finish and engraving, especially of some of the guns from Italy, is outstanding. Do not have any hesitation, therefore, if you are faced with the possibility of buying a foreign gun.

For a first gun, a beginner should place himself in the hands of a reputable gun-dealer. He will have a wide range of guns, both new and secondhand, he will know exactly what you should have once you have explained your requirements. If of sufficient standing he may have his own shooting ground where the gun, or a variety of guns, can be tried and the ultimate choice fitted. Make sure that he is a member of the Gun Trade Association; as such he has a reputation to maintain and will do his utmost to see that you are matched to the gun that meets both your purse and sport.

Don't negotiate with the local sports shop which happens, amongst the athletic gear, to have a dozen or so guns. It is unlikely that you will receive the expertise or attention which is so vital.

What of the secondhand market? Well, good guns and excellent bargains can be acquired through the classified columns of the sporting press, or even the local newspaper, whilst auction rooms are a happy hunting ground for bargains. The proviso is, however, that you must know exactly what you are up to. Never purchase a gun without having it vetted first by a competent gunsmith. It may, to your unskilled eye, appear the bargain of the century but initial appearances can deceive. Damascus barrels can be blacked to hide their tell-tale pattern and probable black powder provenance; a loose, rattling action can be tightened to camouflage its worse defects, though the first box of cartridges may disclose its true condition; the proof marks, though indicating that the gun was originally proved for nitro, may mask the fact that the barrels are now way out of proof, either through excessive use or through having been lapped. Only a gunsmith or an expert used to handling dozens of guns will be able to tell at a glance, and a quick measure of the barrels with the gauges will reveal the true condition and value of a secondhand gun. Of course, you may be fortunate, but reduce the risk by obtaining a second, expert opinion before buying it.

Having, we hope, discovered a gun which appears to meet our requirements, a gun which may be English or foreign, new or secondhand, try to gauge its quality and 'feel'. This is by no means as simple as it may appear. Just as it takes considerable time and experience before a horseman can assess an animal, so it demands a good many guns through one's hands before one can instantly identify that 'something' which marks a gun as a thoroughbred. Heft it between both hands, is it well balanced and does it come smoothly to the shoulder and align with a target whilst you keep both eyes open? Is it cast correctly for you? I.e., is the stock bent just sufficiently to ensure that the barrels are in line with your vision and the target?

Above all, take time when buying a gun. There are hundreds of models on the market, available through a variety of sources and in a multiplicity of conditions so you have ample opportunity to play the field. Impulse buying, the secondhand dealer's friend, should be avoided at all costs.

The importance of placing yourself in the hands of a competent gun-dealer cannot be over-emphasized. He it is who will make certain that the gun chosen between the two of you, fits you like a glove. Remember that most guns can be altered to suit your requirements. An excess of choke can be removed and stocks altered to meet your physique.

If, from the start of your shooting career, you have a gun that fits, the battle is more than three parts won. Assuming that you are put together like a reasonably normal human being with average reflexes and sight, then there is every reason why you should become a competent shot.

One area so frequently overlooked is care of the gun. You have just purchased a fairly expensive chunk of wood and metal which, given adequate attention, should see your life out. But remember that you will be shooting under a variety of conditions, from warm, sunny days with dust in the air to bitter marshland mornings when salt and rain may be a major hazard. Luckily we no longer have to worry about the corrosive effects of black powder, though it is always advisable to clean one's barrels immediately after shooting despite the claims for non-corrosive cartridges. Obtain a cleaning rod (the old-fashioned jointed kind are best), a screw-on mop for oil and a phosphor bronze for removing traces of leading, though be sparing with the latter as too vigorous use may score the barrel. There are a variety of oils on the market but you cannot beat Three-in-One oil and a spray such as WD40. If the gun is wet, first dry the barrels, fore-end and stock with a warm dry towel and then go over it carefully with either blotting paper or absorbent tissue. Run the edge of the paper along either side of the rib and take particular care round the trigger guard and top-lever. When you are absolutely certain that every drop of moisture has been removed, the barrels can then be cleaned.

Everyone who shoots has his own 'special' method of barrel cleaning; mine is to roll balls of absorbent toilet paper, placing one in each chamber. These can then be pushed through the tubes with the cleaning rod in one continuous sweep. You will probably discover that the barrel now appears spotless, and if so fix the wool mop to the rod, lightly oil and give the tubes a good polish. Finally, I spray WD40 as a protective. If, however, you discover leading — grey streaks in the barrel — these can be removed by using the phosphor bronze. The outside of the barrels can be lightly oiled. Run an oily rag over the lockwork but make sure that no oil penetrates the wood round the action. Oil here can lead to swelling in the woodwork.

If the woodwork is muddy or salt-caked, wash it off with warm, soapy water, dry it thoroughly, then rub in a small amount of linseed or one of the stock preparations on the market.

Keep your gun stored upright in a security cabinet, not in a case. The latter should only be used for travelling.

6
Safety

I have seen someone killed in the shooting field, killed by a man who had always preached the rules of safety but who, in the heat of the moment, took a chance – the result of that chance was a man dead with a bullet through the heart. In Great Britain, fortunately, we have a reputation second-to-none for safety but even so, each season, accidents are reported with, occasionally, a fatality.

The two basic tenets to remember at all times where the shotgun is concerned is that at short range its effect on the human body is devastating and that a gun must at all times be treated as though it is loaded. Accidents are caused only by guns pointing in the wrong direction and being fired inadvertently or without sufficient care.

I repeat – consider every gun to be loaded and never, at any time, point it at anyone. If these simple rules are followed accidents simply cannot happen.

Whenever you pick up a gun, or are handed one, even though you are perfectly certain in your own mind that it is empty, open it and check the chambers, making certain that as you do so your finger is outside the trigger guard. Before shooting, you should always squint up the barrels to be sure there is no obstruction in them, such as mud or a piece of cleaning material. Any such obstruction, even snow, could cause a burst barrel, or at best, a severe bulge. This also is one reason why I dislike mixing the company of 12- and 20- bores, for it is all too easy to slip a 20-bore cartridge into a 12-bore chamber only to push in another 12-bore cartridge. The resultant explosion will almost certainly remove a few fingers if not an entire hand.

It is salutary for the beginner to grasp the essentially violent and lethal nature of a 12-bore at close range. The layman has little conception of the power of such a combination and it is little wonder that the shotgun is the preferred weapon of soldiers for close work. To drive home the lethal character of a shotgun it is only necessary to fire at, say, a large tin can at 10 yd (9 m); translate the effect to the soft tissues of the human body and one will begin to understand just how dangerous a shotgun can be if it is mishandled. Remember too, that pellets can ricochet and numerous accidents have been caused by pellets bouncing off a hard surface.

At an angle of 45° a charge of shot may carry a full 200 yd (180 m) and while, at this range, the pellets will be widely dispersed, one single pellet could still put out an eye.

In the field, there can be only two safe ways of carrying a gun – with the barrels pointing either to the sky or the ground. To achieve this, you can carry the gun either through the crook of the arm with the barrels pointing at the ground or over the shoulder with the trigger guard uppermost. Never have the guard down as the barrels will then be horizontal. Never carry the gun at the trail or across the body so that the barrels again point horizontally. Regrettably, you all too frequently come across these last two transgressions. Nothing is more alarming than to walk on the left of someone whose barrels are pointing directly at your midriff. Never have the slightest hesitation in pointing out such potentially lethal acts of stupidity. On the continent, it is a frequent practice to carry the gun over the shoulder, broken and held by the barrels. Perfectly safe, but it is a sloppy-looking method which is seldom adopted here in the field, though clay shooters seem to find it satisfactory.

If you are walking and expect a shot, carry the gun at the high port, with the butt resting against your hip and the barrels pointing at the sky.

Never, at any time, lean a gun against a car, gate or any object from which it might be knocked, perhaps by a dog rushing past. Not only is the gun likely to be damaged, but it is conceivable that, if you have been criminally careless and left it loaded, the safety catch might be jarred off and the gun discharged. Remember that the safety catch is only a safety precaution; the gun can be fired if the catch is slightly at fault or jars off.

When firing a shot, the safety catch should be pushed forward by the thumb as the barrels are raised. This action will eventually become automatic though initially it will require conscious thought.

In the field, there will be numerous occasions when you have to cross an obstacle. Whatever it may be, a fence, hedge, gate or ditch, unload the gun before attempting to cross. If you have a companion, allow him to cross first while you hold both guns, having made sure they are unloaded. Then, after a further check to be certain the chambers are empty, close the gun and hand it across to him by the barrels; do the same with the second one.

On formal driven shoots it is still the fashion amongst an older generation to carry their guns closed between drives, on the specious excuse that *they* know they are empty, rain might get in the action and strain might be put on the latter by the open barrels. Such excuses for a dangerous practice should be treated with contempt. An open, empty gun is safe; closed there is no guarantee that it does not have a cartridge in the chamber. It may not

The effect of 11/16 oz (30 g) of No 6 shot fired at a can from a few yards away. Imagine the effect on soft human tissue.

Always check the chambers.

The right way to carry a gun on the shoulder . . .

. . . and the wrong way.

Never carry a gun at the trail.

Correct way to carry a gun when not shooting.

Wrong — but often seen! Barrels point at next gun in line.

Right — gun at high port when walking.

Left: *All set for an accident.*

Below left: *Crossing a fence: Wrong . . .*

Below: *and right.*

be convenient to carry your gun broken if you are travelling in a Land-Rover between drives, but there is nothing to stop you clearly indicating to the other sportsmen that your gun is empty before you close it.

It goes without saying that accidents in the shooting field are more likely to occur when a number of people are gathered together in reasonably close proximity. The solitary wildfowler is likely to place only himself in danger through inadvertently blocking his barrels with mud, whereas the driven game shot has to think not only of his neighbours on either side of him, but also of the advancing beaters and the pickers-up to the rear.

You may never shoot driven birds but if you do find yourself tackling pheasants, partridges or grouse under these circumstances bear in mind the two strategic safety areas – the ground immediately in front of you and the air above. Never take a shot in front which is not well up and beware of woodcock in particular. Flickering outside the covert, they have a deceptive tendency to fly low, and they also create a ripple of excitement amongst the guns.

If there is potential danger in front, then the line of guns on either side of you is even more vulnerable, so never, never swing through or across the line. If you intend to take a shot behind – and make sure it is a high one – then turn with your gun pointing to the sky and held in the high port position, it should not be in your shoulder. Grouse moors are notoriously dangerous in this respect. The birds are low, they will sweep across the line of butts often at head height and it is all too easy for the excited and nervous beginner to lose control and swing through a pack, and through the next butt. Many moors now insist on having poles erected on either side of a butt to act as a physical and psychological barrier to the gun. If you want to take a shot behind in a grouse butt, swivel with the gun at the high port; don't turn with it pointed at the ground as an accidental discharge in a stone-lined butt can produce some extremely unpleasant ricochets.

The rough shooter with one or two companions has an even greater burden of responsibility. It is essential that at all times he knows precisely where his companions are. Has one gone slightly ahead on the far side of a tall hedge? Has one lagged behind in thick cover so that a snap shot at a rabbit could have fatal consequences? And always keep a wary eye on gundogs working with you. Too many dogs have been shot as they emerged ahead of the guns, perhaps in pursuit of a rabbit. Few things are more ghastly than to wound or kill your own or a companion's dog, yet it is surprising how often this happens.

The simple rule – never shoot where you cannot see – applies at all times. A snap at a bolting rabbit could connect with a courting couple. All right, they shouldn't be there, but if it comes to a court case it's you who will be held responsible.

And whilst on this subject, don't neglect to take out third party indemnity. If, however, you are wise enough to join the British Association for Shooting and Conservation (BASC) then you will automatically be indemnified for up to £500,000.

As far as safety in the home is concerned, it should be unnecessary to emphasize that guns and cartridges must *never*, at any time, be accessible to children or those who are neither qualified nor legally at liberty to handle them. Each year, without fail, there will be one or two deaths or severe mutilations caused to children quite simply because a criminally stupid parent either propped a loaded gun in a corner or left it and cartridges where the lethal combination could be triggered off by an inquisitive child.

The only sensible answer is to make sure that guns and ammunition are stored at all times, when not being used, in a police-approved security cabinet. There are a variety of models on the market and well padlocked and bolted to the wall they will provide peace of mind for a moderate outlay.

I hope that you will never be the cause of an accident or near accident in the field. It is perhaps the most frightening and appalling sequence of events. Make certain that you understand fully the deadly and lethal nature of the gun you are handling; use commonsense and never, never take a chance. If you do, nine times out of ten you'll get away with it. On the tenth occasion someone, perhaps a close friend, may be killed or maimed.

7
How to shoot

The theory behind successful shooting at live quarry or clay targets is simple. By making an allowance for the speed and angle of flight of the target and by allowing for possible drift, and the minute fraction of a second for the brain's command to fire to be obeyed, it is mathematically impossible to miss. Fortunately, however, theory and practice are poles apart. How boring and unsatisfying it would be if, each time we fired, we knew there was no chance of missing!

Let's examine, briefly, the basic mathematics of the problem. Shot leaves the muzzle of the gun at a nominal velocity of 1,070 ft (325 m) per second, maintaining this speed over a relatively short distance. It is clear that, whatever speed the bird or target is moving at, it is necessary that the charge of shot should intercept its flight path so that the two elements coincide. To do this, it is essential that the muzzles of the gun are ahead of the target by a distance predetermined by its speed. For example, using a standard velocity cartridge, i.e., 1,070 fps (325 mps), the formula is as follows:

Range	30 yd	35 yd	40 yd	45 yd	50 yd
	(27.5 m)	(32 m)	(35 m)	(41 m)	(45 m)
Forward	5 ft 6 in	6 ft 8 in	8 ft	9 ft 6 in	11 ft 1 in
allowance	(1.7 m)	(2 m)	(2.4 m)	(2.9 m)	(3.6 m)

In the past, books on shooting have often published these tables, solemnly warning the shooter that he must shoot a certain distance ahead of a bird travelling at such-and-such a speed if he is to achieve any success. This, of course, is lamentable rubbish. Sufficient that you understand the theory but don't try to put it into practice.

The chief problem for the beginner is the ability to assess range. As we have already discovered, although the theoretical killing range of the 12-bore is about 50 to 60 yd (45 to 55 m), in practice 40 to 45 yd (35 to 41 m) is the absolute maximum killing range, unless we are dealing with a heavily choked magnum which is being used with a massive load, perhaps 1½ oz (42 g), of shot.

So we really have to work within a 45 yd (41 m) range, whilst it is a fact that the majority of shots taken, whatever the game, will probably be within 20 to 25 yd (18.3 to 22.8 m).

Try to gain some idea of the size of a bird at varying distances; set up a pigeon or pheasant at 10 yd (9 m) intervals up to 45 yd (41 m) so that you can begin to acquire some sort of a mental image of its size in relation to these distances. Watch feral pigeons flying over an object whose height you know. I recall seeing pigeons flying level with the 120 ft (36.5 m) tower at a well-known clay school. At 40 yd (35 m) one would have sworn that they were out of shot! It is a fact that game has to be very high indeed before it is unkillable, yet time and again experienced shots will tell you that pheasants, perhaps flying over a steep valley, were way out of shot when perhaps they were 40 to 50 yd (35 to 45 m) up.

Inland, and especially where there are trees, it is not difficult to assess range quickly; on the foreshore, however, where there is a lack of any physical object in the landscape to provide a reference scale, range assessment becomes very difficult. Mallard at 60 yd (55 m) look like teal at 40 yd (35 m), whilst geese are incredibly deceptive. Beginners all too frequently fire at geese at 100 yd plus, hoodwinked by their size into supposing they are very much closer.

Shooting cannot be taught through the written word; one can only guide and point out pitfalls which must be avoided. It is in the field, with a qualified teacher standing at your shoulder, that the hitherto complicated and mysterious instructions on lead, follow through and swing suddenly make sense.

There are several methods and schools of shooting practice – the Robert Churchill method, the Percy Stanbury school, the conscious forward allowance devotees. Each will argue with vehemence that his is the only practical and consistent method; meanwhile the 'natural' shot will just get on with it, pulling his birds down with consummate ease, yet quite incapable of telling you how he does it if quizzed.

There are, I believe, certain basic elements common to any successful method of shooting. Firstly, as I have before emphasized, the gun must fit so that as it is mounted and slides into the shoulder, the barrels will automatically be aligned on the target. Both eyes must be kept open; no rifle shooting practices here, please! Both eyes, too, must remain centred on the target so that the barrels are not consciously observed, though in the case of a side-by-side the dark lines on either side of the rib will play an important, though not dominant role, by acting as a sub-conscious sight.

46

Above: *Judging range on the foreshore can be deceptive.*

Right: *Correct gun mounting is essential.*

Both eyes must be kept open.

Your weight will normally be on the forward foot, the gun will be balanced between both hands and as the target or bird is seen, the gun will be smoothly pushed into your shoulder with the barrels pointing at the target throughout this action. As the butt beds firmly into your shoulder, with both eyes open and looking hard at the target, touch the trigger. The safety catch will be pushed forward as the gun starts its progression into the firing position. Keep the left hand well forward; this is the hand that will point at the target and ensure that the barrels do so as well. Keep your head well up and make sure that at no time does it drop over the stock; if it does the barrels will be canted.

What about forward allowance? Shouldn't one be working out how far ahead of the target to fire? Not so! Providing your basic stance and gun mounting is correct, forget all about lead and simply fire at the target. One's natural acceleration of swing will ensure that the barrels overtake the bird even though the mental order to fire is given when the barrels apparently point directly at it. This method works admirably for all birds within reasonable range; however, for very high birds — 40 to 45 yd (36 to 41 m) — you will consciously have to push the barrels way ahead of the bird and, frankly, only experience will teach you how far.

The finest shots invariably make the whole business look so easy and unhurried and this, of course, is the secret. With the balance of an athlete, they are capable of using the minimum effort to achieve maximum effect.

It is salutary to stand behind a line of guns at a pheasant shoot. Watch the man who is persistently behind his birds or is wounding them; notice how he mounts his gun the moment the bird appears and tracks it with the barrels but never really catches up with it. The brilliant shot, however, the man who is clipping his birds in the head and killing them outright, appears scarcely to move until the last possible moment and then seems to flick the gun casually at the bird, the barrels moving in a tiny arc. Nevertheless, his barrels have been following the bird's progress, the gun only being mounted at the last moment.

The 'natural' method of shooting is undoubtedly the best. It is, although he or she is unaware of it, the method adopted by the complete beginner who, with some basic instruction, is allowed ten shots at a simple, going-away clay. His mind uncluttered with theory, he will simply pick up the gun, load it and smash clay after clay. Why shouldn't he? It is such a simple thing to do. Merely point the gun at the moving clay and fire. Again and again it works. Yet the moment the boy or girl starts to think and worry about forward allowance, he or she will go to pieces. I've seen it happen time after time.

And that's why I suggest that your best course is to hie you to the nearest clay club or school and place yourself under the instruction of a really good teacher. Remember, though, that an ability to shoot straight does not necessarily carry with it the means to impart instruction. Many clubs, however, now have their own CPSA qualified coaches.

8
The law

As far as Great Britain is concerned, the law relating to the acquisition and use of shotguns is not particularly difficult to comprehend and in its execution is, on the whole, applied impartially.

Firstly, what is a shotgun? For the purposes of the Firearms Act 1968, it is defined as a smooth-bore gun having a barrel not less than 24 in (600 mm) in length and not being an air-gun. A shotgun with a barrel length of 24 in (600 mm) or under falls within the Part One Firearms Act and requires a Firearms Certificate.

Before you can acquire or have in your possession a shotgun you must be in possession of a shotgun certificate.

The only exceptions are the following. A shotgun certificate is not required for the possession of component parts of a shotgun. Nor is it required if:

(1) you have been in Great Britain for not more than thirty days in all in the preceeding twelve months; the purpose of this exception is to allow over-seas visitors to land in this country with shotguns for short visits without obtaining a certificate;

(2) if you use a shotgun at a time and place approved for shooting at artificial targets by the Chief Officer of Police for the area in which that place is situated;

(3) if you hold a Firearms Certificate issued in Northern Ireland which authorizes you to possess a shotgun;

(4) if you borrow a shotgun from the occupier of private premises and use it on those premises in the presence of the occupier.

In order to obtain a shotgun certificate, you must apply for a form from your local police station and assuming that you do not already possess a Firearms Certificate (issued for rifles or handguns) the information you are required to produce must be verified by the signature of a second party who must have known you for at least two years, be a British subject and not a member of your family, and who must be a Member of Parliament, Justice of the Peace, Minister of Religion, doctor or person of similar standing.

The Chief Constable is under an obligation to issue a certificate unless the applicant is prevented by the Firearms Act from possessing a shotgun as a result of a prohibition applied for certain criminal behaviour, or if the police believe the applicant cannot be permitted to possess a shotgun without danger to the public safety or peace.

The applicant must, on receiving his certificate, sign it with his usual signature and also inform the police immediately of the theft or loss of any shotgun in his possession.

The shotgun certificate allows the holder to have as many guns as he may require in his possession. It is not necessary for any gun to be specified, nor has the Chief Constable any right to specify where the gun may be used, to impose conditions on its use or to require particular safety measures to be taken in the home before issuing the certificate.

A shotgun certificate lasts for three years and currently costs £12 on first application and £8 on renewal.

Although, as stated above, there is no compulsion on the part of the applicant to ensure any specified safety precautions, today only a fool will fail to take the most elementary measures to ensure that a gun cannot be readily stolen or handled by children. As mentioned in the chapter on safety, I would recommend that you purchase a gun security cabinet, of which there are many models on the market, and make sure that it is securely bolted to the wall. If it is provided with heavy padlocks and possibly linked to a household security system, then at least your conscience is clear. It is a fact that even today guns are still left lying round the house where children can find them – even more terrifying is the fact that they are sometimes left loaded!

As far as age limitations are concerned, a child aged less than fifteen must not have an assembled shotgun with him except while under the supervision of a person at least twenty-one years old or while the gun is so covered with a securely fastened gun cover that it cannot be fired. Youngsters of fifteen or over may have assembled shotguns without either of these restrictions. A person may make a gift of a shotgun or shotgun ammunition to a youngster aged fifteen or over but not to one under fifteen.

Having obtained your shotgun certificate and, we assume, a shotgun, you may now legally shoot clay targets, certain creatures categorized as pests throughout the year and other birds within specified seasons.

In order to kill game you must also possess a game licence, which can be taken out annually at a post office for a fee of £6 if taken out after July and before November and to expire on 31 July, or to be taken out after July and before November and to expire on 31 October for a fee of £4, or to be taken out after 31 October and to expire on 31 July, again for £4 or for any continuous period of fourteen days for £2. A gamekeeper's licence is £4.

In order to kill game, you must have a game licence.

Game is defined as pheasants, partridges, grouse, ptarmigan, capercaillie, blackgame, woodcock, snipe, hares, deer and, with certain exceptions, rabbits.

Wildfowl, i.e., geese, duck and the wader which may be legally shot are not considered game nor do they require a game licence.

Certain close seasons have been laid down by law during which quarry species may not be shot, killed or taken. The open seasons are as follows:

pheasant	1 October to 1 February
partridge	1 September to 1 February
grouse	12 August to 10 December
capercaillie	1 October to 31 January
ptarmigan	12 August to 10 December
woodcock	1 October to 31 January
snipe	12 August to 31 January

Cormorants are now protected.

Geese and duck may be shot from 1 September to 31 January above and on the foreshore, but there is an extension of twenty days for these birds to 20 February below high water mark of ordinary spring tides.

The wader which may be shot is the golden plover. Its open season is from 1 September to 31 January, but with no extension into February.

The geese which may be shot are: Canada geese, greylag, pinkfoot and whitefronted geese. This last in England and Wales only.

The legal duck are: mallard, wigeon, teal, pintail, tufted, pochard, shoveler, gadwall and goldeneye.

The following species are protected but subject to a Special Licence if they are causing damage: cormorant, shag, goosander, red-breasted merganser and barnacle geese.

Shotguns are illegal against deer.

Apart from the statutory close seasons game may not be killed on a Sunday or Christmas Day nor may you take or destroy any game at night.

Where rabbits are concerned, a game licence is normally required, the only exceptions applying to certain categories of person under the Ground Game Act of 1880. Under this Act the occupier of land has a right, of which he cannot be divested or divest himself, to kill hares and rabbits on his land. Only he and persons authorized by him in writing have that right and do not require a game licence. Such authorized persons are:

(1) Members of his household resident on the land in his occupation.
(2) Persons in his ordinary service on such land.
(3) One other person only, bona fide employed by him to take hares and rabbits for reward.

Nor may you kill rabbits or hares by firearms at night. The only exception is a landowner in occupation with his sporting rights in hand.

As far as deer are concerned, the recent Wildlife and Countryside Bill has made it illegal to use a shotgun on deer. There are one or two exceptions, but these need hardly concern the average shooter. The day of the hideous deer drives to shotguns is now ended. A shotgun should never be used on deer, other than with solid ball, for which a firearms certificate is required — and your chance of obtaining that is nil. Deer should only be killed by those who have specialized knowledge and who use the correct calibre of rifle.

Statutory close season for deer (All dates inclusive)

Species	Sex	England/Wales	Scotland
Red	Stag	1 May to 31 July	21 October to 30 June
	Hind	1 March to 31 October	16 February to 20 October
Fallow	Buck	1 May to 31 July	1 May to 31 July
	Doe	1 March to 31 October	16 February to 20 October
Roe	Buck	1 November to 31 March	21 October to 20 April
	Doe	1 March to 31 October	1 March to 20 October
Sika	Stag	1 May to 31 July	1 May to 31 July
	Hind	1 March to 31 October	16 February to 20 October

9
Game

Pheasants

By virtue of its widespread distribution, its sporting character and the fact that it can be reared on a large scale with the minimum of fuss, the pheasant must be considered the premier sporting bird, though doubtless pursuers of grouse and grey partridges would question this.

The pheasant is not a native of this country but is believed to have been introduced by the Romans; this was probably the blackneck type, though there is, I believe, a mosaic in Britain depicting the typical ring-neck pheasant. The bird is found throughout the entire British Isles with the exception of very high ground, mountains and open moors. Originating from China, it is an habitué of marshy ground, though will adapt to almost any form of agricultural practice. The only truly wild pheasants I have shot have been rousted out of thick Norfolk reed-beds and in character and appearance are very different to their reared cousins. Small, dark and swift, they are quite at home in the wettest of conditions, preferring to fly only a short distance and then drop back into the reeds. The majority of so-called wild pheasants were probably reared and released by man one or two generations back.

Today's pheasant wears a coat of many colours. He may be the traditional ring-neck, he may lack the ring, he may be a so-called Chinese bird with almost white wings, he may be a melanistic, a magnificent bird of deep glowing purple and green, or perhaps the latest fad, the 'Bohemian', a drab buff-coloured bird, which, crossed with the traditional colour, produces a hideous chequered creature. The weight of the average cock pheasant will be around $3 - 3\frac{1}{2}$ lb (1.3 – 1.6 kg) and the hen $2 - 2\frac{1}{2}$ lb (0.900 – 1.1 kg). However, every season 'monsters' of $4\frac{1}{2}$ or over 5 lb (2 – 2.3 kg) are recorded.

In the wild the hen nests in April to May, incubation lasting twenty-three to twenty-six days; the average clutch is about ten or eleven eggs, though this may vary up to sixteen or seventeen. There is sometimes a tendency for two or more hens to lay in the same nest, so producing huge and unhatchable clutches.

Pheasants, on a large or small scale, can be reared with comparative ease, provided that certain sensible precautions are observed. Assuming that, perhaps, you would like to try your hand at backyard rearing, to produce, say, fifty or 100 birds for your shoot, you can use either a small incubator (there are now many on the market) or, preferably, half-a-dozen broodies. The latter, though difficult to obtain, are well worth the effort. If you intend to produce a regular supply of poults for your shoot it is well worth acquiring a small flock of hens for broodies. Avoid the modern hybrid varieties which have had all the broodiness bred out of them, and instead try to obtain a silkie-cross light Sussex or Rhode.

The art of rearing game is quite fascinating, teaching one a great deal about the birds, the diseases to which they are subject, and how they adapt to the wild. For further information on this subject you cannot do better than apply to the Game Conservancy for one of their famous Green Booklets, which deal with the subject in depth.

Typical ring-neck pheasant.

Pheasants can be walked-up, usually over spaniels or pointers, or driven. Each form of shooting has its merits and each, like all things, can be open to abuse. There is little point in blasting a low-flying pheasant in the backside at 15 yd (13 m); it is an absurdly easy shot and the end result will be inedible. Allowed to get out and rise, such birds can provide excellent shooting, particularly if they are spiralling up through a network of branches. Similarly, low and slow-driven birds are not worth the cartridge, quite apart from the safety factor; but a high hen screaming off a hillside with the wind in her tail is a very different proposition. Curling and sliding, she will test the most expert shot and only those who have tackled such birds will know just how difficult they can be.

Red grouse

Let's scotch one myth straight away. For a long time writers have claimed that the red grouse is unique to this country and is found nowhere else. This is simply not true. Our grouse, formerly labelled *Lagopus scoticus,* is today regarded merely as a distinct dark race of the willow grouse *(Lagopus lagopus)* and has been re-christened *Lagopus lagopus scoticus,* a bird which has a wide range across America and Eurasia. However, unlike its northern cousin it never turns white in the winter. There are probably in the region of half a million grouse pairs in Britain and Ireland today, the chief habitat being from Yorkshire northwards to include much of Scotland, the emphasis being on the east and central parts. However, grouse are also found in Wales and south along the Pennines to North Staffs whilst a handful eke out an existence on Exmoor and Dartmoor where they have been introduced.

In appearance the red grouse is a rich, deep brown with a hint of red, barred and spotted with white and black on the undersides. The legs are fully feathered and the cock has prominent red 'eyebrows'. The average size is about 15 in (380 mm) from beak to tail and it weighs about 1½ lb (680 g).

The great advantage of the grouse is that it is a truly wild bird, responsible entirely for its own reproduction. However, moor management is essential if a healthy and vigorous population is to survive. It is now known that the composition of the soil plays a vital role in the size of a grouse population. High densities occur over base-rich rocks such as diorite and epidiorite, rocks which increase soil fertility and thus the nutrient value of the heather, the principal food of grouse.

The moor keeper must ensure that the heather remains in suitable condition for grouse; the birds prefer young ling heather shoots and in order to sustain a steady supply the moor must be burnt in carefully selected patches each season, so that a healthy young growth can emerge. Grouse

The red grouse is not unique to Great Britain.

also require grit to help grind their food so the keeper must also see that piles of grit are available.

Fluctuations in grouse populations are due either to disease, severe weather, or a combination of both. Late frosts can 'brown' the heather, leaving birds to suffer from malnutrition, whilst the weak birds will succumb to the strongyle worm which is present in all grouse. Ticks and coccidiosis are additional health hazards, both of which encourage virus diseases.

Incubation usually starts in early May and lasts between twenty-four and twenty-seven days, the average clutch being in the region of ten to twelve eggs. The chicks at first eat insects so it is essential, if they are to survive, that a reasonable spring has ensured a good supply of insect life.

Grouse are normally shot in one of three ways in this country. They can be driven, and this usually applies to the big, highly organized moors with a suitable stock of birds; they can be walked-up, a somewhat haphazard method, or they can be dogged, i.e., shot over pointers or setters.

If you are sufficiently fortunate to be invited to shoot driven grouse you will experience the cream of shooting. The birds are fast, very fast; they are low and hug the contours, and will probably be on you before you are alive to the fact. The essential rule to recall when shooting driven grouse, as emphasized in the chapter on safety, is that whilst you can shoot both in front of and behind your butt, never swing across the line of butts as a pack of grouse sweeps across. Always try to take the first bird at least 40 yd (36 m) in front. Mark your fallen birds, don't allow your dog to pick up during a drive; don't shoot in front when the beaters appear within 200 yd (183 m) and try to remain calm and unflustered. It won't be easy!

Shooting grouse over pointers or setters is sheer delight. The shots will not be difficult, you will not have so many as with driven birds, but you will be able to watch dog-work at its best. To see a brace of red setters, English pointers or German short-haired pointers working a moor, to watch them on point, rock steady as a covey bursts into the air in front of them, is truly privileged shooting.

Ptarmigan

These delightful mountain grouse demand a special effort on the part of the shooter; seldom found below the 2,000 ft (610 m) mark and native only to the Scottish Highlands, some tough, physical exertion is required if one is to make a bag of half-a-dozen or so.

Of the grouse family, the ptarmigan is a master of camouflage, moulting constantly throughout the year to ensure perfect background coloration. In summer the bird is a subtle mixture of grey body and white chest and wings but in the winter it becomes pure white with black outer tail feathers. The average weight is about $1\frac{1}{4}$ lb (0.567 kg).

It is virtually impossible to drive ptarmigan, they can only be walked-up. I have shot them once only, an exhausting foray with snow on the ground and a blizzard raging. The birds burst from the hillside, almost at one's feet, like hurtling snowballs, launching themselves straight off the side of the mountain.

Blackgame

The blackcock, the male bird, is a truly magnificent grouse; glossy black with a lyre-shaped tail and a white powder-puff of feathers beneath it, he is a trophy, in full plumage, worthy of the taxidermist's art. The female, a drab lady of mottled greys and light browns, is known as a greyhen. These large

Ptarmigan shooting on the high ground.

Blackcock at the lek.

grouse – the cock will weigh about $3\frac{1}{2}$ – 4 lb (1.6 – 1.8 kg), the hen $2\frac{1}{4}$ – 3 lb (1 – 1.3 kg) – were once widely distributed and even in the last century could be found on the heathlands of Surrey. Now, apart from a handful believed to exist in the West Country, they are to be found on the edges of moorland from the north of England through to Scotland.

Blackgame are deceptively fast; don't be deceived by their size and apparently slower wing-beat than grouse. They are usually encountered whilst shooting a moor for grouse, the likely spots to find them being small valleys or gulleys clothed in birch and scrub. Be very careful at the start of the grouse season – blackgame are out of season until 20 August and there may be young birds mingling with grouse and looking deceptively like them.

In the spring, the males gather at a traditional 'lekking' area where, with tails displayed over their backs, they circle and dance for the benefit of the females. Incubation is about twenty-seven days, the nest containing six to ten eggs.

Capercaillie

This, the biggest of the grouse family, is an impressive bird both to shoot and to handle. The cock, weighing up to 12 lb (5.4 kg) is a greeny-blue-black with a brown back, red wattle and hooked beak; the hen is mottled reddish-brown and weighs in the region of 7 – 8 lb (3.2 – 3.6 kg).

Found only in the pine forests of Scotland, its principal food is buds and shoots of conifer and for this reason some shooting men claim that it is inedible, the turpentine in the shoots imparting a tainted flavour to the flesh. However, if the crop is removed immediately, they taste excellent.

The capercaillie became extinct in the early nineteenth century, but was re-introduced into Perthshire with breeding stock from Sweden. It is now spreading, taking advantage of increased afforestation.

The nest is usually little more than a scrape in the ground containing from five to ten eggs, laid in early May. Incubation is twenty-seven to twenty-nine days.

In this country capercaillie are invariably driven, but on the Continent where they are considered to be a prize game bird, they are frequently stalked and shot with rifles. A driven cock caper is an awesome sight, flying with uncanny speed and silence and proving extremely deceptive as it swoops downhill. Don't be deceived by the size of the bird into supposing it is nearer than it is. Large shot, say No 4 or 5, is necessary.

Grey partridge

A favourite with most shooting men, the grey, or common, partridge is a true native of this country, found throughout the British Isles with the

Capercaillie . . . Britain's largest grouse.

exception of high ground. The most favoured areas have traditionally been the east of Scotland, East Anglia and the southern counties, in particular Hampshire.

A brown bird with russet head, cream barrings and light underparts with a chestnut horseshoe mark on the breast, usually but not invariably more strongly marked in the cock bird, the partridge weighs about 12 – 16 oz (340 – 453 g).

Forming a pack or covey through much of the year, the birds will pair off in January, or later if the weather is really hard. The number of eggs laid varies considerably, though an average clutch is probably in the region of twelve to fifteen. Incubation starts in mid-May, the traditional time for the hatch being mid-June.

The fortunes of the grey partridge have fluctuated in the past two decades, and whilst there have been seasons of promise, on the whole the grey partridge has been in severe decline. A number of causes have been advanced but it is likely that a combination of factors – removal of hedgerows, increased use of pesticides, the spread of silage and a series of disastrous breeding seasons – have been responsible. A vast amount of research has been, and is being, undertaken by the Game Conservancy into the factors affecting the grey partridge and some of the answers now being proposed may help to ensure a future for this, the most charming and exciting of game birds.

In the early part of the season coveys can be walked up with moderate success, the birds bursting from the stubbles like exploding star shells. Beginners are more often than not caught off balance as the birds whirr into the air; they may seem simple shots, but it is all too easy to shoot at empty air, panicking to get off two shots before they are out of range. The experienced shot will deliberately pick his two birds and refuse to be distracted by the others. The usual mistake made by a novice is to 'brown' the covey in the vague expectation that something, somewhere, must fall. It rarely succeeds, and even if it does, is unsporting.

Driven grey partridges, if shown well, provide really testing shooting, particularly if they are driven over high belts. On spotting the guns they will swerve and curl, so that it is a good man who can calmly take his right-and-left.

Red-legged partridge
The red-leg, or Frenchman as it is sometimes called, was introduced into this country in the latter part of the seventeenth century. A larger bird than the grey partridge, it is readily distinguished by its olive back, red bill, white eye-stripe and barred sides. Whilst cocks usually have a small spur or knob on the back of the heel, this is not invariable and cannot be used as a

definitive guide to sex. Cock birds, however, are larger and more aggressive-looking than hens. Rearing habits are similar to the grey partridge, though the cock may also incubate the eggs.

Red-legs have always had a bad reputation in the shooting field, being more inclined to use their legs than to take to wing. However, once airborne they fly fast and well, though more inclined to rise singly, rather than pack into a covey.

Widely reared and presenting few problems to the keeper, they are usually treated on a put-and-take basis, rather like pheasants. It is generally considered that they nest in the wild only sporadically, so that the population on a shoot must be topped up each year.

Woodcock

Although, like the snipe, a wader, the woodcock is treated as a game-bird. Long beaked, with a large, liquid eye, soft, feathered round wings, the 'cock is a fascinating mixture of russet autumnal shades. The bird will weigh 9 – 14 oz (225 – 395 oz) and measure perhaps 1 ft (300 mm) or more from beak to tail. There is a resident population but this is augmented in the late autumn by birds from the Continent, moving across the country from east to west, often coinciding with the full moon in November. Found wherever there are boggy, scrubby patches or thickets of rhododendrons, it may also occur literally anywhere according to the weather.

Woodcock have a reputation for causing rather more than a ripple of excitement and, on an organized driven shoot in particular, may prove a safety hazard as they loop and skim at head height in and out of the edge of a covert. In the open they are not difficult to shoot but in coverts dodging through the trees, they can baffle the best of shots.

Year after year woodcock will return to the same haunts and in some parts of the country, particularly the west, their predictability on suitable terrain can result in quite impressive bags. However, on most shoots half-a-dozen birds in a day is more usual.

Don't forget to remove the pin-feathers from the wrist of each wing to adorn your shooting hat! At one time it was thought that the flavour of the bird could be improved if the sinews of each leg were drawn as soon as the bird was shot but this is now largely discounted.

And by the way, if you have the fortune to shoot a right-and-left at woodcock you can claim membership of the exclusive Bols Snippen Club plus a tie and a bottle of their famous liqueur!

Snipe

Although three species of snipe may be encountered in this country, only one, the common snipe, is legal quarry, though until the 1981 Wildlife and

Countryside Bill the diminutive jack snipe could also be shot. The third snipe is the great or double snipe, larger than the common and very unlikely to be encountered. The little jack snipe has a very different flight pattern to the common snipe, flying in a straight line and seldom more than 50 yd (45 m) before dropping back into cover, though almost indistinguishable if driven. The common snipe may be found almost anywhere in Great Britain where marshy, wet conditions prevail, though, as with the woodcock their movements and numbers relate to the weather. Cold, freezing conditions will send them scurrying in search of soft feeding.

There are two schools of thought as to how snipe should be shot when they are walked-up. One maintains that they should be walked down-wind so that, on rising, they have to turn into the wind thus presenting a relatively easy shot, before they dart away in typical zig-zag fashion, whilst the other prefers to walk them up-wind as they can then often be approached closer.

Frankly, I have never found a great deal of difference, preferring in either case to let the bird get out well before firing. Fire too soon and you may well shoot at a zig when the bird is on a zag! There is a definite art to snipe shooting and only those who have shot a great many know the secret.

Snipe can be driven and providing they are in the marsh in good numbers and the wind is right, really great sport can be had as they hurtle over like darts. Although I have shot snipe with No 6 shot, 7s or 8s are preferable. The bird only weighs 6 oz (170 g) and you need a dense pattern to ensure a kill.

Snipe do breed in this country but the great majority of birds in the winter come from abroad, hard weather on the Continent often sending them across the water in considerable numbers.

10
Wildfowl

Mallard

The three duck most likely to be encountered by the novice shot are mallard, teal and wigeon in that order. Mallard – the traditional wild duck – are to be found almost throughout the British Isles, on lakes, dykes, streams, ponds, marshes and rivers: on high ground, on low, and on the foreshore or stubbles in September. Weighing in the region of $2\frac{1}{2}$ lb (1.1 kg) to just under 3 lb (1.3 kg), the mallard is familiar to everyone – the drake with its glossy green head, white neck ring and curly black tail, the duck with her mottled brown plumage. Both have bright orange legs.

In the early part of the season, before the September stubbles have been ploughed in, mallard can provide superlative sport as they flight in to feed on the loose grain as dusk closes on a warm, early autumn day. You will have to reconnoitre the area for a week or so before you shoot, but once you are certain of your quarry a hide in a hedge or a bale hide in the field itself with decoys on the stubble, will be sufficient to give you the chance, if all goes well, of half-a-dozen fat mallard. At no time of the year are they better suited for the table, having gorged on grain. As with all hide shooting, remember that the wind will dictate the birds' approach. They are likely to swing down-wind to spy the ground and then, if satisfied, make the landing approach into the wind. The ideal is then to have them coming at you with paddles down.

Mallard can be shot from the edge of dykes, rivers and pools, they can be flighted on the foreshore, on inland floods or into flight ponds.

Many shoots now rear mallard to supplement the pheasant shooting. The first big pheasant day on the majority of shoots is not until the end of October, when the birds are flying well and leaves are beginning to fall, so it is convenient to fill in with one or two flights at the duck in the early part of the month. This is fine provided that the duck are kept wild. Shoots that allow their duck to become tame bring the sport into disrepute. Nothing is more unpleasant than seeing half-tame mallard being knocked out of the sky as they circle their home pool at head height.

Flighting mallard.

Teal

This, the smallest duck in the British Isles, has a fast, exhilarating flight.
Like the mallard it may be found almost anywhere from the foreshore to
inland pools and gutters. Weighing under 1 lb (450 g) the cock teal has a
rich fox-red head with cream stripe above the eye, grey vermiculated back
and flanks, speckled chest and green speculum. The hen is a dowdy brown.
Both have grey legs.

Teal can offer tremendously exciting shooting, especially at evening
flight, over a fed-in pool or wild splash in the water-meadows. If there is a
wind they will speed past, perhaps in a pack of twenty or more, swerving,
rising and falling, the cocks uttering a thin plaintive piping.

Wigeon

Until relatively recent times, wigeon would normally only be encountered
on the coast. But with the decline of their traditional food, *Zostera marina*,

they have turned to inland waters, favouring areas of winter flooding where they can dibble for weed-seeds and grasses. The Cambridgeshire Washes are a famous haunt of wigeon, thousands filling the empty skies when conditions are right, the cock birds wheeooing and the hens giving vent to a purring growl.

The wigeon is a plump duck, weighing perhaps $1\frac{1}{2}$ lb (680 g). The cock has a handsome chestnut head with yellow crown, grey vermiculated back and flanks, pinkish chest and white belly. The hen is a rich, dappled brown, also with the pure white belly.

Like teal, wigeon are truly wild duck and must be sought in the more desolate places. The finest shooting is, perhaps, at night under a full moon and cloudy sky when, on foreshore or inland, they may come in their dozens to a favourite splash.

A pack of wigeon dropping in to feed on inland grass.

69

The Canada goose is now found throughout the UK.

The geese

The beginner is, quite frankly, unlikely to encounter the grey geese that are legal quarry unless he is fortunate enough to be included in a serious fowling trip to Scotland or perhaps the Wash. Of the grey geese, only pinkfeet and greylegs can legally be shot in Scotland, though to both these species can be added the whitefront in England and Wales. The Canada goose can be shot throughout the British Isles.

The grey geese will normally be shot, either at morning or evening flight on the foreshore or an inland lough or lake, or else when they flight to feed during the day. Often easily decoyed, large numbers can be destroyed under these circumstances, though only a greedy fool would shoot more than half-a-dozen or so. Bags of 100-plus have not infrequently been made over decoys, something of which no sportsman should, or could, be proud.

The beginner is far more likely to come across the massive Canada goose. Weighing up to 16 – 17 lb (7.2 – 7.7 kg), this grey-brown goose with black and white head, black neck and white breast, frequents grassland close to lakes or reservoirs and is unpopular with farmers due to the damage it can cause to crops, not so much through the amount it eats but by virtue of the fact that it 'paddles' and flattens the young corn.

These geese, introduced some 200 years ago, have a very strong hold in the Thames Valley where hundreds can be seen. Like all the geese, they can be shot at dawn or evening flight. Remember that they are massive birds and call for heavy shot. A right-and-left at Canadas is unforgettable as they plummet into the edge of a lake, sending up plumes of spray! If it is a question of food, try to avoid shooting the leading bird as this will probably be a gander, wise, elderly and tough to boot. Young Canadas are particularly good on the table; never be deterred by the fairly irksome chore of plucking them. The end result is well worth the effort.

11
Rabbits, pigeon and various

For the beginner and the rough shooter, rabbits and pigeon have always provided a staple diet incorporating excellent sport with good food. Rabbits, for years, could be relied on for ferreting, trapping, snaring, shooting and long-netting. Country lads could learn not only the rudiments of sport but acquire a real understanding of the countryside and its ways in their pursuit of the rabbit.

Rabbits
Sadly, for some twenty years after the first outbreak in Kent in 1954, the rabbit population was so reduced by the disgusting disease myxomatosis that those who loathed the rabbit were able to speculate with glee on its possible complete eradication from this country. But they had reckoned without the stalwart character of this little immigrant (the rabbit is not a native to this country but was probably brought over in Norman times); wily and resourceful, small pockets of rabbits built up a resistance to the disease, an immunity which was apparently passed on to succeeding generations. Gradually the worst ravages of the disease were reduced so that, today, whilst not yet back to pre-disease numbers, rabbits have built up a healthy and thriving population, once again offering sport and food to a new generation of sportsmen. Certainly, there are still outbreaks of myxomatosis – the disease is carried by the rabbit flea – but these seem to occur only in the autumn and are swiftly extinguished.

Rabbits can, of course, be shot in a variety of ways. Where they are particularly prolific they can be stunk out of their burrows, using creosoted paper a day or so before the shoot, and then driven with dogs to a waiting line of guns. Such a method, frequently used in the old days when there were sufficient rabbits and labour force to justify it, might result in huge bags being taken. For instance, in 1898 five guns shot, in one day, 6,943 rabbits in eight hours; Sir Victor Brooke, in 1885, killed 740 rabbits to his own gun in one day, firing exactly 1,000 cartridges – he also shot from his left shoulder for half the day and then switched to his right!

Rabbit shooting, using spaniels, can be very exciting but certain precautions must be taken. If there is more than one gun, know exactly their location and never move without letting them know. Before you shoot check your safe line of fire on either side and behind and be extremely careful where dogs are concerned. Never, ever take snap shots at movements in the undergrowth – it may be a rabbit but there could also be a spaniel right on its scut.

Rabbits can, of course, be stalked using a shotgun; dashing from cover in a thick, tussocky old field they can give reasonable sport but I must confess that I can see little point in knocking over sitting rabbits with a charge of

Rabbit shooting can be very exciting.

shot, unless one is desperate for a bunny for the pot or to feed a ferret. There's much more fun and skill to be obtained by stalking with a heavy air-rifle or .22 rifle.

And when you've shot a rabbit, what then? Always carry a hunting knife; it may be a small lock-blade or a belt knife, but be sure that it carries and holds a razor-sharp edge. Do not waste your money on long-bladed Bowie-type knives. They are virtually useless in the field. A good grip combined with a 2 or 3 in (50 – 75 mm) drop-point blade is all you need.

It is best to paunch rabbits on the spot, though before doing so press the lower part of the animal's belly, rubbing your thumb towards the scut, to clear the bladder. Hold the rabbit between your legs, head up, and make an incision from the breast-bone to the hind legs, being careful not to cut the entrails. Pull the skin apart, then make another cut through the membrane covering the entrails. Now take hold of back and forelegs and with a flick of the wrist eject the entrails. You will then have to insert two fingers behind the stomach to pull this free. Hock the back legs by cutting behind the heel of one leg and inserting the other through the incision. Rabbits cleaned thus should be hung as soon as possible for cooling.

The quickest way to skin a rabbit is simply to cut the skin in the middle of the body, right over the back, so that the skin is in two halves. Take hold of each and pull sideways – lo and behold! a skinned rabbit. Quarter your rabbits and pop them in the deep freeze. You'll then have a ready supply of really delicious meat.

Pigeon

Woodpigeon can offer some of the very finest shooting this country has to offer. They can be shot as they flight in to roost, walking up the edge of woods or rides or over decoys on a variety of crops in summer or winter. They can be ridiculously simple, dropping in to a pattern of decoys on a hot summer afternoon with wings spread as they lazily drift down, or they can prove the better of even the most accomplished shots, weaving and darting through and over the bare February woodlands with a gale in their tails.

The biggest bags will usually be made over decoys and this type of shooting, brought to perfection by 'professionals' such as Archie Coats and David Home-Gall, has developed into a sport in its own right. So much so that the modern shooter, pursuing pigeon over decoys, can find himself so cluttered with equipment, some of it quite unnecessary, that he will require a small van to convey it all to the shooting ground. If you feel your sport will be improved by using wing-flappers, complicated hides or lofting poles, well and good. You may obtain immense satisfaction from pulling strings or carting vast quantities of paraphernalia.

The biggest bags will usually be made over decoys.

I believe that the basics are essential if you are determined to make a bag of pigeon. You must have convincing decoys. This is especially true today, for there is not the slightest doubt but that pigeon, having been hammered for a number of years, are increasingly wary. There was a time when any old decoy, perhaps even a bottle painted grey with white marks, would draw birds but that seldom applies now. The best decoy is a dead bird, its head propped up and feathers smoothed. If you're likely to have several decent days' decoying, keep back a few birds in the deep freeze, from each expedition. Stuffed birds are too expensive and very difficult to carry. There was a fad, for some years, for dead birds injected with formalin. These, if correctly prepared, were light but fragile, requiring a special carrying box. Of the artificial decoys, without a shadow of doubt the best are the Double-H decoys made from soft rubber, with a balloon inside the body to keep it rigid. I have seen pigeon settle amongst a spread of these decoys, quite convinced that they are genuine. There are, of course, numerous other decoys on the market; choose wisely and avoid like the plague those with shiny paint. The decoy should have a matt grey finish and the white marks on neck and shoulders must be distinct. These flashes are the signals, seen by pigeon from a distance, which act as magnets.

You will require a simple, portable hide. There are several on the market or you can make your own from five light metal stakes, each with a Y at the top and a sharp point plus a right-angle projection 1 ft (300 mm) above the point to help you kick or press the pole into firm ground. A blacksmith will make these up for you. Three of the poles should be about 5 ft (1.5 m) in length and two slightly shorter. Netting can then be draped round the hide and interwoven with natural foliage so that the hide blends with the background. Elderberry bushes are, in the summer, particularly useful; easily cut, the branches help to disguise the hide and are also a good fly deterrent. Quite often, there will be no need for an artificial hide; you can utilize a hedge or ditch or construct a bale hide. A billhook will figure prominently amongst your items of essential equipment, but do not go berserk with it, disfiguring the countryside with glaring white stumps and broken branches scattered willy-nilly.

One of my friends has now dispensed completely with hides. Dressed entirely in camouflage clothing, including face mask and gloves, he reckons to be able to kill just as many birds in greater comfort by merging with almost any background.

It is, within these pages, impossible to do more than touch on the subject. If you are convinced that pigeon shooting is for you then join a local pigeon club, buy one or two of the numerous books which have been published and, above all, understand that pigeon can be incredibly frustrating. Descending in clouds on laid corn or peas day after day, they may have vanished when you attempt to go for that record bag. Very much subject to food patterns, the weather and disturbance, only patience and concentrated effort will reap rewards.

Use No 6 shot under most circumstances, perhaps switching to 1 oz (28 g) of 7s if decoying at close range. There was a time, not so long ago, when it was solemnly believed that woodies could only successfully be defeated with No 4 or 5 shot. The theory was that pigeon absorbed shot, only the heaviest being capable of bringing them down. We now know better, but there is not the shadow of doubt that birds will occasionally continue to fly for quite a distance even though apparently hard hit. Always watch a bird which rocks when you fire. If it settles in a tree within a few hundred yards it will usually be picked up dead under the branches, or it may suddenly collapse, even up to half-a-mile away or more. Such birds will have been hit in the lungs.

Various
It is a scientifically established fact that game and predators such as crows, magpies, jays, stoats, weasels and rats cannot co-exist. The latter will prey on partridges, pheasants and wildfowl at every opportunity – and why

should they not? Each species is determined to thrive and must seize every chance to do so. Regrettably, clashes with the interests of sportsmen and naturalists are inevitable. Practical conservationists are well aware that, left to their own devices, the predators mentioned above will swiftly reduce not only game populations but also those of song-birds, and it has long been recognized that well-keepered woods are of enormous benefit to a wide variety of bird life. So-called sanctuaries in which no predator control is permitted invariably degenerate into vermin-infested strongholds.

If you want to encourage game, you must take every opportunity to destroy crows and ground vermin in particular. Never pass up the chance to kill a crow. Relentless seekers after eggs and fledglings, they can be seen

Weasels must be destroyed in defence of game.

in the early summer quartering the ground in search of partridge and pheasant nests. The evidence is plain to see, each egg having a ragged hole in it. One of the best ways to destroy crows is in the spring when they are nesting. It is possible, with nerve-wracking caution, to creep up on a hard-sitting hen and shoot her as she slips off the nest. The latter can then be blown apart with heavy shot. Intensely curious, crows will sometimes decoy to a dead crow tossed from a hide or to an owl decoy set up on a post within shot of a very carefully concealed hide. In the latter case they are intent on mobbing the bird. Their eye-sight is truly astonishing; they will spot the slightest movement or betrayal of human flesh from hundreds of yards away.

Magpies and jays are most likely to be caught napping on a driven shoot, though even here such is their cunning that on spotting the line of guns they are quite likely to turn back through the beaters or sideways out of trouble. The jay's dipping flight makes it a difficult target as it flits from tree to tree.

Sadly, for they are in many ways delightful little animals, neither weasels nor stoats can be spared and should be shot at every chance. In the spring the keeper, amateur or professional, will have a line of tunnel traps as a defence against both animals and also that revolting creature, the rat.

Today we have another menace to plague and destroy game and wild-fowl. Mink have spread rapidly throughout the countryside, as a result of escapes from fur farms. No birds can exist in their presence and they should be trapped and shot whenever the occasion arises. They have proliferated to such an extent that packs of hounds are being formed, many replacing the otterhound packs now that that sport can no longer continue. They provide grand sport for their followers, quite apart from performing a useful task.

A word of warning: in the past, game preservers had at their disposal a vast array of effective and, frequently, deadly means of disposing of vermin; these included the use of poisons, traps and snares. Today the only traps which are legal must be set under cover and the use of any poison or toxic substance is strictly forbidden. Don't be tempted to 'dope' eggs or to set traps in the open; the use of poison is fraught with danger; eggs or tainted meat can easily be picked up by children or domestic pets and every year a few keepers are caught in this stupid practice. Not only keepers, for some hill farmers, totally indifferent to wildlife, continue to strew poisoned carcases for the ostensible destruction of foxes. Too often, though, a magnificent bird of prey, such as an eagle or kite, falls victim.

Remember that all the birds of prey – hawks, falcons and owls – are protected by law. Their numbers have diminished to such an extent that they deserve all the help we can offer.

12
Gundogs

I cannot imagine shooting without the assistance and companionship of a gundog, quite apart from the fact that, for humanitarian reasons, a dog is a vital part of your equipment. You will inevitably wound the odd bird or animal and the aid of a good dog may be the only means of ensuring that they do not suffer. It is virtually out of the question even to contemplate rough shooting or fowling without a dog. Not only will it retrieve the slain, it will find them in the first place.

As far as choice of breed is concerned there are, in fact, nineteen breeds of working gundog in this country but many are specialized, such as the pointers and setters, and a few are now so reduced in working ability and numbers through social and economic changes plus the attentions of the showing fraternity, that they are hardly worth considering.

The choice lies among the retrievers, spaniels and hunt-point-retrieve breeds. Of the retrievers, the labrador and golden retriever are the best choice for a beginner, of the spaniels the English springer and of the HPRs the German shorthaired pointer.

The basic purposes of these three gundog sections relate to the type of shooting involved. The retrievers are intended to stay to heel, to mark shot birds and to retrieve. The labrador is particularly suitable for the wild-fowler, provided it is the old-fashioned sort of dog, heavy of bone with a thick otter tail and a substantial undercoat. Regrettably the labrador has tended to decline in recent years into a whippety creature, light of bone with a thin tail, sharp-set head and a habit of galloping over its nose. Labradors are also suffering from several endemic diseases such as hip-dysplasia and retinal atrophy. Golden retrievers have advanced enormously in recent years, having great success in trials. Inclined to mature late they are, nevertheless, well worthy of consideration.

Neither of these breeds are really suitable if you are looking for a dog to burst through thick cover, ignoring brambles and thorns and intent only on turning out the rabbits or skulking cock pheasant. For this job the English springer spaniel reigns supreme. This is the dog for the rough shooter who

No-one should shoot without a dog.

Spaniels are ideal for rough shooting.

wants the ground covered within shot, confident that nothing will be overlooked. Springers do, however, require a handler who can keep on top of them. If they know that their handler is likely to let them get away with a modest crime, murder will soon be on their shopping list.

The English springer does enthuse over his job and will keep you on tenterhooks as he covers the ground, determined to find a rabbit on the barest of cover.

The HPR breeds – the German shorthaired pointer, Vizsla, Weimaraner and Large Munsterlander – have only come to prominence since the last war and it's fair to say that of the four the GSP is by far the most popular and, probably, the most accomplished. The breed has three functions – to hunt, to point quarry and to retrieve it when shot. A really good GSP is an absolute joy to shoot over. There is nothing quite as exciting as watching a dog on point, the body rigid, the head pointing at the quarry; to shoot the bird, and to have it retrieved by the same animal combines all the most superior qualities of a gundog.

You may have guessed by now that I'm sold on GSPs! I've owned a labrador and springers, but much as I admire the many excellent qualities inherent in these breeds none have approached the working abilities of my GSP. Besides which he was also the easiest of the three to train!

Having said that, let me emphasize at once that the best breed of dog for the beginner is the one he feels happiest with. Every individual has his or her own ideas on what constitutes, for him, the ideal working gundog. Only experience will endorse or modify that opinion.

Having decided to obtain a gundog, of whatever breed, you must observe a few simple, basic rules. You are about to purchase an animal which will, with luck, serve you for nine or ten years. You must get the best that you can afford – or even the best that you cannot afford! Under no circumstances consider purchasing a 'backyard' breeder's puppy. Such litters are often the result of little thought on the owner's part, merely a desire to 'give the old girl a litter', the sire usually being some local hero whose background may be as dubious as his looks.

Avoid like the plague, any hint of show blood in the pedigree, no matter how many generations back. The show fraternity have done their utmost to ruin our working gundogs by breeding purely for their own absurd standards of 'beauty', neglecting almost entirely the working abilities of the dogs.

Study the columns of the shooting magazines and note the top kennels, take advice from trainers, professional and amateur, and wait, if need be, for the right litter. Don't take any members of your family with you when you inspect a potential litter – they will probably fall for the cuddliest, but not necessarily the best, puppy!

You do not, of course, have to undergo the traumas of puppyhood. Young, hand-trained dogs of perhaps a year to eighteen months can be obtained. It is possible that a kennel with its eye on field trials has a dog or two which would never make the trial scene, but which are perfectly adequate for the shooting man with no great ambitions. These may have been trained to walk to heel, drop to shot and retrieve, but their education needs to be polished. You can also, of course, purchase the finished article, a dog which is ready for the field. Be prepared, however, to pay £150 to £250 for the hand-trained dog and upwards of £300 for the finished article. High prices, you may think, but then a great deal of work and time has gone into producing them. Dogs are no longer cheap – good dogs that is.

If you choose the soft option and can afford to purchase a 'made' dog, do use commonsense before committing it to the field. Far too many dogs, bought from a trainer, are taken out shooting within a week of purchase and expected to perform like a robot. The purchaser never pauses to consider that the dog, at one with and used to the commands of its erstwhile trainer, may be totally at a loss with its new owner. The environment is strange and possibly upsetting so it is little wonder that the dog fails to live up to the high expectations placed on it by its purchase price. You must give the dog at least a month to settle down, to get to know you and to understand your commands. Make absolutely sure, when you buy it, that the trainer provides you with a list of verbal and whistle commands and note carefully how they are used when you see the dog demonstrated.

There is, however, not the slightest reason why you should not train a young dog to a satisfactory level. The basics you must aim for are that it should walk to heel, hunt within range of the gun if required to do so, retrieve tenderly, drop or at least stop to whistle or shot, take to water readily and accept hand signals. Quite a lot you may think, but it is, after all, the basic requirement of any competent gundog and well within the capabilities of any *working-bred* retriever or English springer. If you acquire a GSP then you will also require that it should point game.

There is not space to elaborate on detailed training methods. You cannot do better than to acquire a really good book on the subject: probably the best is the classic work by Peter Moxon, *Gun Dogs: Training and Field Trials* (Popular Dogs).

Today's methods of training are based on commonsense and the ability on the part of the trainer to appreciate that his pupil can only communicate by example; it is the pyschological approach, so very different to the old-time methods of dog breaking, in which the animal's spirit was literally cowed by physical punishment. Try to think like a dog and, above all, don't rush the training. Take it slowly, one step at a time, making quite certain that the pupil has absorbed the lesson before moving on to the next.

Novice trainers have a tendency to become bored with, as they see it, the basics of training such as teaching walking to heel or dropping to whistle or shot. They'd much rather move on to the exciting retrieving part, leaving lessons half taught.

The great secret is to study the mentality of your dog; come to understand whether it is a 'hard' dog, unlikely to be deterred by the sound of shots, the sort of dog that will take advantage of a moment's lapse on your part, or whether it is a soft, easily cowed animal. You must act accordingly. Little and often is the key to basic training. Don't, for instance, overdo dummy work. Ten minutes is usually quite enough and then only two or three times a week.

Above all, try to understand why a dog takes a certain action and see it from its point of view. Be extremely careful when the dog is first allowed to hear a shot. *Never* take it into the field and fire a twelve bore over its head! It may sit there totally unperturbed, but it is far more likely to make a bee-line for its kennel and you will probably end up with an incurably gun-shy dog. Introduce the sound of gunfire from a distance, using a blank pistol, and if you have any reason to suspect that the dog might be nervous, use a little pyschology. Fire the pistol when the dog is about to be fed so that, gradually, it comes to associate the sound with something pleasurable.

The beginner can obtain an enormous amount of help from gundog training classes. These have proliferated throughout the country, enabling the novice to learn how to handle a dog, and teaching the dog itself how to behave in company.

Such classes are usually the first stepping-stone to gundog tests. These have now developed into a major activity throughout the spring and summer months, so much so that they have become a sport in their own right and the 'test' dog has tended to develop.

If you become, as I hope you will, deeply absorbed by gundogs then, who knows, you may well advance into the ranks of the field trialers. Don't be put off by the inevitable sense of mystique which can surround these affairs. The people engaged, professionals or amateurs (and the latter predominate today), are invariably friendly and only too pleased to assist the genuine beginner.

It is a fact that a great many shooting folk gradually find that their interest in gundogs overtakes the sport and numerous pickers-up on shoots much prefer to work their dogs for the benefit of the guns, obtaining enormous satisfaction from a job well done and also from the knowledge that no wounded birds are left behind.

13
Clothing and equipment

Today's shooting man is extraordinarily fortunate. At his behest is a vast range of country clothing, designed to cater for every conceivable sporting contingency, backed up by vast quantities of equipment. You can, however, have too much of a good thing and the chief problem for the man kitting himself for the field is to discriminate between the claims of numerous retailers, most of whom appear to be selling the same item under fanciful names.

The majority of shooting takes place in the winter months, so that the two basic requirements are warmth and waterproofing. Coupled with these must be sufficient freedom of movement to permit you to shoot, and actually move your arms!

If you are wildfowling on a bitter January foreshore or shooting driven pheasants with a freezing wind icing the blood as you wait for a drive to get under way, then you must, in my view, wear some form of thermal underwear in the shape of a long-sleeved vest and long-johns. This type of underwear is a vital part of mountain and trekking expeditions and I can guarantee the pleasurable effect of a really warm inner layer under freezing conditions. I have worn thermal underwear in Canada and Sweden, on hunting expeditions and I blessed every penny spent. I also have a pair of quilted undertrousers which can be worn beneath ordinary trousers but they are rather bulky so in dry but brisk conditions I've worn them to good effect over pyjama trousers. The main thing to aim for is a comforting layer of warm air trapped between the garment and your skin.

Progressing outwards we come to the shirt. This, in the case of driven or rough shooting, when conditions are reasonably clement, can be an ordinary cotton-wool mixture, but for all-round warmth give me flannel or wool, preferably with a long tail to keep the lower part of the back warm. There is also, today, the moleskin material, a brushed, hard-wearing cotton. It is an extremely durable and pleasant material, with a soft feel to it, rather akin to a genuine mole's skin, and it improves as it grows older and gets washed repeatedly.

Depending on the weather, we can now slip our shooter into a sweater and/or some form of quilted-type waistcoat or jacket. The heavy-weight sweaters of oiled wool with genuine suede shoulder and elbow patches are probably the best on the market, but you will find that they tend to prove bulky under a jacket, unless it is cut very loosely round the arm-pits.

Quilted jackets can be obtained in a bewildering variety of shapes, colours, styles and materials. Cut with plenty of stretch, in green or fawn, the majority are perfectly adequate for year-round shooting, except when it is bitterly cold or raining. None claim to be more than shower-proof, but all are comfortable and smart.

One of the finest materials for shooting, and in particular woodland deerstalking, is Austrian loden cloth. Made from untreated sheep's wool, so retaining the natural grease, and normally featured in a dark green, loden cloth is tough, warm, soft and silent. I emphasize silent because so many of the man-made fibres rustle alarmingly. Loden is virtually water-proof, unless you break the surface tension. But for 100% waterproofing there is still nothing to beat waxed Egyptian cotton. This material, first introduced with such success by Messrs Barbour of South Shields with their thornproof clothing, has never been surpassed. No countryman can be seen today without his thornproof if the weather looks threatening. The wildfowler, in particular, owes an enormous debt to the thornproof – the famous Solway Smock being almost standard and indispensable fowling gear for the foreshoreman.

For extremely cold and hard conditions – again I have tested this in Canada – one cannot do better than the 'Igloo' coat made by Pakamac of Lancashire. Cut long, with heavy duty zip and large fur-lined hood and various other refinements, it is the ultimate in protection and warmth – but not suitable for a quiet potter round the shoot for a pigeon!

As for your legs, well to some extent the formality of the shooting dictates the nether regions. For instance, driven or walked-up days demand the almost universal plus-twos in some form of tweed, needle-cord or mole skin. They are extremely comfortable to wear and if of a stout tweed will repel all but the most torrential downpours or a slog through wet kale.

They must be worn with heavy wool stockings and you can then choose either leather or rubber boots. I have now discarded the once ubiquitous green wellington boot for the greater comfort of, preferably, leather boots or front lace-up, calf rubber boots. The best in my cupboard is a pair of supple leather boots from Toronto, every seam welded and stitched and with a sole designed to take the effort out of walking.

Whatever type of footwear you choose, make quite certain that it fits perfectly, supports your ankles and will not rub your calves. Ill-fitting footwear can mar a day's sport, or it can make it.

The wildfowler must, of course, invest in a pair of thigh-boots. Take my advice and get the full length ones rather than the three-quarter length. I would also opt for the black, fisherman's type rather than the lighter but less substantial green ones. They may be suitable for anglers but do not stand up to the wear and tear of the foreshore.

You will also have to obtain a pair of over-trousers. Dripping wet kale and brambles or a steady drizzle will soon penetrate all but the toughest of tweeds and although, again, there is a wide range of over-trousers on the market, you cannot do much better than a pair of the waxed cotton over-trousers which button down the sides. Avoid flimsy nylons or materials which are likely to snag and tear on thorns or barbed-wire.

The pigeon shooter and ferreter may opt for the comfort and camouflage of some form of parachute smock; a visit to your local army surplus will usually reveal a wealth of camouflaged items of clothing, including hats. For summer pigeon shooting by the edge of corn I find my old safari jacket perfect, being light and blending with the background.

Headgear is really a matter for the individual and one of the few ways he can express his individuality. You can have fore-and-afts, deerstalkers, floppy inexpressibles, peaked affairs or smart caps. Or you may prefer a trilby which, with time, age and neglect will acquire a distinctive air – not to mention aroma!

Rain, however, still has a nasty habit of trickling down one's neck, no matter how snugly fitting your collar and I cannot recommend highly enough the absorbent cravat sold by the incomparable Cambrian Flyfishers Ltd.

Gloves present a problem. Woollen affairs reduce the tactile contact with the gun and I only wear them under the most bitter conditions. A compromise is the mitten, which does at least keep the wrist warm while the fingers turn blue. The best gloves I ever had were of supple, thin leather lined with silk. They fitted like a second skin and were incredibly warm . . . and expensive!

There are now four major pieces of equipment required – a large, well-constructed game-bag, with a removeable, washable lining and a net container on the outside, and a broad canvas strap which is adjustable; a cartridge bag to contain at least 100 cartridges, again with an adjustable strap and secure fastener; a cartridge belt to hold thirty or so cartridges (the best will have enclosed bottoms to each loop so that cartridges all remain at the same level); and a gun sleeve. This is extremely useful on driven days between drives, ensuring that your gun does not get knocked in the Land-Rover, and remains reasonably dry if the day is wet. The best are of leather, lined with wool and with heavy-duty zips, but there are a variety in canvas or some form of nylon, many of which are excellent value. When using a slip be quite certain that the end is tightly secured; failure to check will mean that one day your precious gun may slide out, butt first onto hard ground.

My only other essential is a good pair of binoculars for pigeon shooting or wildfowling; mine are 10 × 50, but 8 × 30 is quite adequate. Rubber armouring is a bonus that is well worth looking for. I always carry a hunting knife on my belt and whether you choose this fashion or a pocket knife, you will find it essential. The advantage of a belt knife is that you know exactly where to find it, whilst pocket knives have a habit of vanishing. Pick a knife with a short blade and drop point.

Finally, keep your clothing and equipment in good order. Repair rents to clothing at once and wax your thornproof jacket every year (you can purchase the wax for this from the manufacturers) whilst boots, if leather, should be kept supple with neatsfoot oil, lanolin or beeswax. Keep a fine edge on your knife with an Arkansas stone and touch the blade with a drop of oil before replacing it in its sheath at the end of the day. All leather, whether on your game or cartridge bags or gunslip, must be oiled regularly.

Useful addresses

Today's shooting man, particularly if he is taking up the sport, must appreciate that there is a small but extremely vociferous and well-organized opposition to *all* field sports. Until recently hunting bore the brunt of attacks from the opposition to field sports – 'antis' for short – but there is now a concerted campaign to ban all forms of live shooting, and even fishing. The shooting man, whether he lives in the heart of the countryside or the middle of London, must now be prepared to stand up and defend his sport. No longer can he sit on the sidelines, allowing the foxhunters or beaglers to absorb the shock – some of it is coming his way.

Without the slightest doubt, the wisest course is to join either, or preferably both, the British Field Sports Society or British Association for Shooting and Conservation. The former has an extremely active and efficient parliamentary lobby whilst the latter deal specifically with all aspects of live shooting. BASC, in addition, provides an extremely important Third Party Liability Insurance cover up to £500,000 whilst you are engaged in shooting, conservation work and gamekeeping.

Arms and Armour Society,
40 Great James Street,
Holborn, London WC1.

Association of Masters of Harriers and
   Beagles,
John Kirkpatrick,
Fritham Lodge,
Lyndhurst,
Hampshire.

Association for the Protection of Rural
   Scotland,
20 Falkland Avenue,
Newton Mearns,
Renfrewshire G77 5BD.

Birmingham Gun Barrel Proof House,
Banbury Street,
Birmingham 5.

Bols Woodcock Club,
Rozengracht,
103 Amsterdam,
Netherlands.

British Association for Shooting and
   Conservation,
Marford Mill,
Rossett,
Wrexham,
Clwyd LL12 0HL.

British Deer Society,
The Mill House,
Bishopstrow,
Warminster,
Wilts.

British Falconers Club,
P. T. Fields,
3 Orchard Lane,
Longton,
Preston PR4 5AY.

British Field Sports Society,
59 Kennington Road,
London SE1 7PZ.

BFSS (Scotland),
Glenmore Lodge,
Moffat,
Dumfriesshire.

British Pistol Club,
251 Hurst Road,
Sidcup,
Kent.

British Sporting Rifle Club,
7 Grove Gardens,
Frimley,
Camberley,
Surrey.

British Trust for Ornithology,
Beech Grove,
Tring,
Herts.

British Waterfowl Association,
Market Place,
Haltwhistle,
Northumberland.

Central Committee of Fell Packs,
O. C. D. Berry,
Ellergreen,
Burneside,
Kendal,
Cumbria LA9 5SD.

Clay Pigeon Shooting Association
   (CPSA),
107 Epping New Road,
Buckhurst Hill,
Essex 1G9 5TQ.

Council for the Protection of Rural
   England,
Hobart Place,
London, SW1.

Country Landowners' Association,
16 Belgrave Square,
London SW1.

Falconry Centre,
Newent,
Glos GL18 1JF.

Fell & Moorland Working Terrier Club,
John Winch,
6 Ascot Road,
Shotley Bridge,
Co. Durham.

Forestry Commission,
231 Corstorphine Road,
Edinburgh EH12 7AT.

Game Conservancy,
Burgate Manor,
Fordingbridge,
Hants.

Game Farmers' Association,
S. Jervis-Read,
Walnut Tree Farm,
Charing,
Ashford,
Kent.

Gun Trade Association,
K. Topping,
22 Park Gate Road,
Cannock Wood,
Rugeley,
Staffs WS15 4RN.

Hawk Trust,
The Secretary,
PO Box 1,
Hungerford,
Berks RG17 0QE.

Irish Clay Pigeon Shooting Association,
20 Butterfield Drive,
Rathfarnham,
Dublin 14.

(Irish) Field and Country Sports
    Society,
M. C. A. Jackson,
Cooleven,
Manor Avenue,
Greystones,
Co. Wicklow.

Irish Masters of Foxhounds
    Association,
R. de V. Hunt,
Rockmount,
Kilmacthomas,
Co. Waterford.

Irish Masters of Harriers Association,
R. N. Craigie,
Knockanally House,
Donadea,
Naas,
Co. Kildare.

Kennel Club,
1 Clarges Street,
London W1.

London Proof House,
The Gunmakers Company,
48 Commercial Road,
London E1.

Masters of Basset Hounds Association,
Rex Hudson,
Yew Tree Cottage,
Haselton,
Northleach,
Glos.

Masters of Deerhounds Association,
E. R. Lloyd,
Honeymead,
Simonsbath,
Minehead,
Somerset.

Masters of Foxhounds Association,
A. H. B. Hart,
Parsloes Cottage,
Bagendon,
Cirencester,
Glos.

Masters of Otterhounds Association,
J. Williams,
Upper House Farm,
Hascombe,
Godalming,
Surrey.

Muzzle Loaders Association of Great
    Britain,
Hon. Sec.,
30 Park Road,
Hampton Wick,
Kingston-upon-Thames,
Surrey.

National Coursing Club,
35/7 Grosvenor Gardens,
London SW1W 0BS.

National Rifle Association,
Bisley Camp,
Brookwood,
Woking,
Surrey.

Nature Conservancy,
19-20 Belgrave Square,
London, SW1X 8PY.

Red Deer Commission,
J. Dooner,
82 Fairfield Road,
Inverness.

Royal Society for the Protection of
    Birds,
The Lodge,
Sandy,
Beds.

St Hubert Club of Great Britain,
1 Whitehall Place,
London SW1A 2HE.

Scottish Clay Pigeon Association,
42 Hill Street,
Tillicoultry,
Clackmannanshire.

Scottish National Coursing Club,
Joan W. Davidson,
2 Bungalow,
Eastriggs,
Annan,
Dumfriesshire.

Scottish Shooting Council,
1 Saxe Coburg Place,
Edinburgh.

Shooting Sports Trust Ltd,
22 Park Gate Road,
Cannock Wood,
Rugeley,
Staffs WS15 4RN.

Ulster Clay Pigeon Shooting
    Association,
6 Springhill Avenue,
Hangor, Co. Down.

Welsh Clay Pigeon Shooting
    Association,
Trefrane,
Roch,
Haverfordwest,
Dyfed.

Wildfowl Trust,
Slimbridge,
Glos.

World Pheasant Association,
Daw's Hall,
Lamarsh,
Bures,
Suffolk CO8 5EX.

Index

Page numbers in italic refer to illustrations.

action, *25*, 26

Barbour of South Shields,
    Messrs, 84
barrels, 25, *25*
    cleaning, 37
binoculars, 86
blackgame, 10-11, 60, *61*, 62
Bols Snippen Club, 65
bore, 25
Boss and Woodward, 23
boxlock action, *24*, 26
British Association for
    Shooting and
    Conservation (BASC)
    (*formerly* Wildfowlers'
    Association of Great
    Britain and Ireland), 8,
    12, 21, 44, 87
British Field Sports Society,
    87
Brooke, Sir Victor, 71
Browning guns, 22, 23

Cambridgeshire, 15-16
Cambridgeshire Washes, 69
capercaillie, 11, 62, *63*
cartridge bags, 85
cartridge belts, 85
cartridges, *28*, *29*, 28-34
chambers, 25
choke, 26, 29-30
Churchill, Robert, 46
cleaning, gun, 37
clothing, 83-6
Coats, Archie, 73
cormorants, *53*
coverts, pheasant, *15*, 16
crows, 76-7
curlew, 54

decoys, use in pigeon
    shooting, 74, *74*
deer, 54, *55*
Dickson's round action, 26
dogs, gun, 78-82
double snipe, 66
driven game shooting,
    safety and, 43, 60
drop-down guns, 22, *23*
duck, 11, 54, 67-9

English springer spaniel,
    78, *80*
equipment, 85-6

Firearms Act 1968, 50
Firearms Certificate, 50
footwear, 84-5
fore-end, 26
Forestry Commission, 11

game bags, 85
game birds, 56-66
Game Conservancy, 57, 64
game licence, 51, *52*
geese, 11, 13, 54, 70, *70*
    Canada, 70, *70*
    grey, 70
    greyleg, 70
    pinkfoot, 70
German shorthaired
    pointer, *78*, *80*
gloves, 85
golden retriever, 78
Green Booklets (Game
    Conservancy), 57
Ground Game Act 1880, 55
grouse, 10-11, 43, 58-60, *59*
gun dogs, 78-82, *79*
*Gun Dogs: Training and
    Field Trials*, 81

gun sleeves, 85-6
Gun Trade Association, 36

hares, 30, *31*
Harkom, Joseph, 24
headgear, 85
hide shooting
    mallard, 67
    woodpigeon, 75
Home-Gall, David, 73

jays, 77

knives, hunting, 86

labradors, 78
law, shotguns and the, 50-5
Lincolnshire, 15-16
loden cloth, 84

magpies, 77
mallard, 11, 67, *68*
melanistic pheasant, 56
mink, 77
Monte Carlo stock, 26
mountain grouse *see*
    ptarmigan
Moxon, Peter, 81
myxomatosis, 71

nitro proof marks, 34

open seasons, 52, 54
over-and-under guns, 23,
    24, 25

Pakamac, 84
partridges, 7-8, *8*, 62, 64-5
    common, 7, 62, 64
    French, (red-leg), 7-8,
        64-5
    grey, 7, 62, 64
pens, release, 16, *17*

pheasants, 10, 56-8, *57*
  blackneck, 56
  Bohemian, 56
  Chinese, 56
  ring-neck, 56, *57*
pigeons, 10, 18-19, *19*, 73-5, *74*
pistol-gripped stock, full, 26
  half, 26
plover, golden, 54
pointers, 78, 80
Powell and Sons, William, 23
proof marks, 34
ptarmigan, 11, 60, *61*
push-rod bolt, 26

rabbits, 9, 18-19, 55, 71-3, *72*
range, assessment of, 45-6, *47*
rats, 77
rearing, pheasant, 57
red-legged partridge *see* French partridge
redshank, 54
release pens, 16, *17*
release woods, 16
Remington guns, 22
repeaters, 22-3
retrievers, 78
rough shooting, *12*, 13, 43

safety, 38-44, *40*, *41*, *42*

safety catch, 26-7
Scotland
  capercaillie, 11
  ptarmigan, 11
  wildfowling, 12
seasons, open, 52, 54
second-hand guns,
  purchasing of, 36
shoots, locating, 14-21
shot, lead, 29, 30
shotgun certificate, 50-1
shotguns, 22-7
shotting patterns, 29-30, 32, *33*
side-by-side guns, 23, *23*, 25-7
sidelock action, 26
snipe, common, 65-6
  great, 66
  jack, 66
Solway Firth, 12-13
Solway Smock, 84
spaniels, *12*, 78, *79*, 80
springer spaniel, 78, 80
Stanbury, Percy, 27, 46
stoats, 77
stock, gun, 26
straight hand stock, 26
'superpose' over-and-under gun, 23

teal, 68

Thames Valley, 70
thermal underwear, 83
thornproof clothing, 84
Three-in-one oil, 37
traps, vermin, 77
triggers, 26
trousers, 85
true cylinder, 29

underwear, 83

vermin, 77

WAGBI, 8, 12, 21
wading birds, 54
Wash, The, 12-13
weasels, *76*, 77
wigeon, 68-9, *69*
wildfowl, 67-70
Wildfowlers' Association of Great Britain and Ireland (WAGBI) (*now* British Association for Shooting and Conservation), 8, 12, 21
wildfowling, 8, 9, 11-13
Wildlife and Countryside Bill 1981, 65-6
willow grouse, 58
Winchester guns, 22
woodcock, 65
woodpigeon, 10, 18-19, *19*, 73-5, *74*